H.

HOPE
AN INVITATION

SR. JOSEPHINE GARRETT, CSFN

Our Sunday Visitor
Huntington, Indiana

Nihil Obstat
Msgr. Michael Heintz, Ph.D.
Censor Librorum

Imprimatur
✠ Kevin C. Rhoades
Bishop of Fort Wayne-South Bend
April 19, 2023

Our Sunday Visitor Publishing Division
Our Sunday Visitor, Inc.
200 Noll Plaza
Huntington, IN 46750
www.osv.com
1-800-348-2440

ISBN: 978-1-63966-040-7 (Inventory No. T2790)
1. RELIGION—Christian Living—Inspirational.
2. RELIGION—Christian Living—Personal Memoirs.
3. RELIGION—Christianity—Catholic.

eISBN: 978-1-63966-041-4
LCCN: 2023942260

Cover design: Tyler Ottinger
Cover photo by Emily Alexander
Interior design: Amanda Falk

PRINTED IN THE UNITED STATES OF AMERICA

To the people who call me Toni

CONTENTS

1

THE PROBLEM
WITH HOPE

*Today it is not enough to reawaken hope
in individual consciences; it is necessary to
cross the threshold of hope together.*

— *Pope St. John Paul II*

I am a woman full of hope. Let me repeat that, just for my own benefit: I am a woman full of hope. I am also a native Texan, a daughter, a niece, a sister, a youngest child, a godmother, and a friend who, in my closest friendships, definitely "friended up." I am a religious sister, a member of the congregation of the Sisters of the Holy Family of Nazareth, and also a licensed counselor. Throughout this book, I will share about all those parts of myself. Right now, though, I want to focus on the hope that informs all that I am and do.

My hope did not come cheap, and if you want to see me get real feisty real fast, imply that authentic hope is cheap or false. I remember a boss of mine once looked at me when I was conveying hope in what seemed like a dire situation and said, "Your hope is false." I immediately had one of those flash forward scenes play in my mind: Me flying across her desk in a perfectly horizontal line with my arms stretched out toward her. Why do I get snarly and scrappy when someone tries to undermine or dismiss hope? Because for many years, I was not a woman full of hope. I was terrified to hope for much, and I didn't even realize it. I can say now that I am a woman of hope, and that I know the value of hope, precisely because for a long time, I struggled to hope.

What do I mean by hope? To explain that, I will begin with a story. I have always been in awe when people make lifelong commitments. I will stare with my eyes wide and my mouth slightly agape as finite people say, "I will love forever"; "I will give my life to my spouse"; "I will be a priest of Jesus Christ forever"; "I will be the spouse of Jesus Christ forever." On November 21, 2020, I said, "I, Mary Josephine, of the Espoused Mother of our Eucharistic King, make the vows of chastity, poverty, and obedience, forever." The reason I stand amazed is because the only life we can bank on is the life contained in the one breath we just drew. It is the most precious gift, the present moment. So, when we make a lifelong commitment, we say, "Whatever breaths I have — whether it is one or one trillion — they are yours." It is absurd, in a way. It is also beautiful and wild. It is the stuff of radical hope. I served as maid of honor once, and I had the groom and bride sign a blank piece of paper at the reception and had it framed. I told them that was all they agreed to that day; that whatever God would write on that paper, they would face it together as spouses.

Authentic hope is powerful. It appears foolish to man, but it is the foolishness of God, and "the foolishness of God is wiser than human wisdom" (1 Cor 1:25). Authentic hope has the power to bring life into complete and utter darkness. Authentic hope is the baptismal font — something that says some oil and water and prayer can alter a person ontologically, making him or her a child of God, marked for eternity. Authentic hope can cause a person raised in poverty to become a world leader. Authentic hope calls a priest to the bedside of a dying person who has spent years with his back turned to God. Authentic hope is the woman who prays for decades that her spouse will be delivered from addiction. Authentic hope makes saints. Authentic hope is best likened to labor pains.

AUTHENTIC HOPE HAS THE POWER TO BRING LIFE INTO COMPLETE AND UTTER DARKNESS.

It was 2009, and I was sitting across from my very first spiritual director. I had started attending spiritual direction after having what was sort of a conversion within my conversion. After being Catholic for four years, I had an opportunity to go to Rome, where I went to Mass and confession at St. Peter's. That trip and that opportunity brought about a deepening of my initial conversion to the Catholic Faith. I wanted to do my part to safeguard and nurture what God had begun in me on that trip, so, among other things, I got a spiritual director. Father Jonathan, my parish priest, was a really fun priest. He was not one of those real polished kinds of priests. (You know the ones who just appear to have it all together and have thousands of followers on social media to boot?) You could tell he did not have it all perfectly together, but you could also tell he was devoted to the ministerial priesthood, come what may. I knew I needed some of that kind of devotion in my life. I knew I would basically always be a hot mess in some way or another, but I wanted to find devotion to Jesus in all circumstances; I wanted to be someone who would not become afraid to show my face in our church when I was struggling.

We had been meeting for a few months, and I was finding the meetings very helpful. One day, we had a lull in our conversation, and he filled the space with a question he had probably asked hundreds of times before to fill lulls: "What's your greatest hope?" I sat there silent for an awkward number of seconds and then began to rattle off something about owning a home and a big promotion. He stopped me and asked the question again, insinuating that I wasn't answering him the right way or that I didn't understand him. I incredulously explained to him that I was a "simple" person (I literally cannot type that and not laugh — if you know, then you know) and just wanted basic things, to work and pay my bills. He pushed. I fell silent as a familiar feeling began to come up. Tears filled my eyes and silence filled the room, as I realized that before a question like "What's your greatest hope," my answers — houses, job promotions, and paying bills — only served to reveal a deeper problem. I didn't hope for much; and I certainly didn't talk to God about great hopes.

I DIDN'T HOPE FOR MUCH; AND I CERTAINLY DIDN'T TALK TO GOD ABOUT GREAT HOPES.

It took me a long time and a lot of therapy to give due respect to pains from my childhood that contributed to my approach to hope, and if that is your case, I want to ask you now to give yourself the gift of acknowledging when a wound is simply scathing. Because sometimes we treat scathing wounds with minimization, and that just doesn't do anyone any good in the long term. My father had struggled with drugs and committed suicide when I was eight years old. I was seven years old the last time I saw my mother, and on that day, she was in the throes of regressing back into her own mental health struggles. To a girl like that, who had lost everything and was too little to name a feeling, let alone actually feel the feelings, hope was risky business. It was risky to simply hope that loved ones would come home when they said they would. So, hope was a business I had given up on, without realizing it.

That day, my spiritual director set me on a path to rediscover hope. But when the veil was pulled back, it wasn't pretty. I'll admit, I was even tempted to return to a life of false hope, because it felt less risky. When studying to be a counselor, I read a case study of a woman who had the veil pulled back on her reality and instead of launching out into the adventure of authentic hope, she simply pulled the veil back in its place and continued to live in false hope and in a false reality. She spent most of her waking hours reliving in her mind a brief affair she had had several years earlier with a much younger man. She began to be seen by a world-renowned therapist who helped to break through the fantasy, and once the fantasy was shattered, she fell into severe depression and did not see much meaning in her real life. Now any therapist would read that and be excited — not because we love severe depression, but because the truth is always the point of departure for sincere healing. The world-renowned counselor was rightfully excited. But shortly after, he received a phone call that the client had made a plan that allowed her to persist in her fantasy and false sense of connection with the man from her past. She returned to her joyful life of fantasy. I do not judge her. It is not easy to look upon a reality we have been hiding from when the veil is pulled back; it's much easier to flee back into our illusions. So, I ask you: What is your greatest hope? Are you playing it safe? Are there some struggles in your life that you avoid facing? Do you avoid having hope in the midst of great struggle? It is OK if you are not able to answer those questions just yet; I realize we are just beginning here.

In recent years, we have gone through a lot as a world, as a country, and as a Church. In so many ways, we are collectively sitting before the reality of a pulled-back veil. So, I offer you these reflections on hope at a time when I think we are each called to a new depth of hope, to discover the courage to not go back, but to press ahead into the unknown. Things won't look perfect with deeper hope; in fact, they might look a little messier at first, because hope and perfection don't go together. But this new depth will be a treasured hope. For the very hope "by which we desire the kingdom of heaven and eternal life" (*Catechism of the Catholic Church* 1817) is the same hope that should be our lens, allowing us to see all that is on earth striving to be as it is in heaven. The promise of a new heaven and a new earth should not diminish "our concern to develop this earth, the expectancy of a new earth should spur us on, for it is here that the body of a new human family grows, foreshadowing in some way the age which is to come" (1049). Ultimately, it is the Our Father "that is the summary of everything that hope leads us to desire" (1820).

When I was invited to write these reflections, I was asked to write a sort of memoir. Yes, this book will be sharing my own story, my own journey with God, with family, with friends, with my sisters. But more than that, it is a reflection on the great problem and the great gift of hope. Our world needs hope. Our country needs hope. Our Church needs hope. Cheap hope will not do. Hope that has not been tried will not do. The hope we need is the kind that can look at the worst of circumstances, at the most difficult people (including whomever I may have deemed my worst enemy), and "hold unwaveringly to our confession that gives us hope, for he who made the promise is trustworthy" (Heb 10:23). We need a hope that shines in the darkness.

2

HOPE IN THE WORLD

We are children of God, and if children, then heirs, heirs of God and joint heirs with Christ.

— Romans 8:16–17

When I was seven years old, my mother sent me and my two older brothers to live with my father. She had worked hard to get some mental health struggles under control, but even at the age of seven, I could see she was fighting a losing battle at that time. I was able to meet with her later in my adult life (that story for another time) and was able to confirm that in the midst of her struggles, she wanted to send us to our dad while she was able to. They had been high school sweethearts but had since separated. We were with our dad for a couple of years, and during that time he was also fighting a losing battle — one I was not able to see so clearly. I would later learn that he struggled with drug addiction and depression, and when I was eight, he committed suicide. My brothers and I were quickly taken in by my aunt and uncle, my father's brother and his wife, Aunt Dee and Uncle Billy. Aunt Dee and Uncle Billy would raise us from that time forward.

We grew up going to church every single Sunday. Sometimes, we were also there on Wednesdays and Fridays — youth groups, choir rehearsals, and so on. So much of our life centered on church, and as a growing young woman, I had no shortage of faith-filled women who were examples for me to follow. I grew up in the Baptist Church, so we shouted and hollered and passed out slain in the Holy Spirit and said amen real loud and dressed extraordinarily well for church. Correction: They shouted and hollered and passed out slain in the Holy Spirit and said amen real loud; I was more reserved, but I did enjoy participating in the exceptional dress. And I loved our church, I loved our way of worship and our music, and I loved youth group. I still cherish that music, and when I feel adrift in my faith, it serves as an anchor. Yet, I had no idea that while I was growing up in the midst of such beautiful faith, I was also harboring a firm resolve that God was not the most powerful person in my life. I thought I was the person most fit to count on. It took until I was grown for that struggle to surface.

WHILE I WAS GROWING UP IN THE MIDST OF SUCH BEAUTIFUL FAITH, I WAS ALSO HARBORING A FIRM RESOLVE THAT GOD WAS NOT THE MOST POWERFUL PERSON IN MY LIFE.

In the meantime, because of the love and sacrifices of Aunt Dee and Uncle Billy, I was able to enjoy a ton of things that "normal" kids get to enjoy, like reading books, hanging out with friends, playing soccer, and singing in church and school choirs. Looking back, though, I can see that over the years, I was growing in insecurity. The kind of insecurity whose seeds are sown in the wound of abandonment — in the shame-ridden wound caused by the lie that says, *They left because something is wrong with me.* I was an insecure middle schooler, an even more insecure high schooler, and a very insecure college student. What did insecurity look like on me? Striving for power and attention. I was far from the mousy, quiet, shy person in the corner because she doesn't like herself. Maybe this will help someone. It is my belief that, in the majority of us, insecurity does not look like sheepishness or shyness. It looks like a carefully deployed shield. Sometimes, the shield is promiscuity or an obsession with physical appearance. Sometimes, it's being the snarky, sarcastic girl who claims to feel nothing and always has a witty quip. Sometimes it's being the angry person; you know the one I'm talking about. On January 1, her Twitter says she's going to be more positive this year, and by noon the same day, she's tweeted three to four complaint-ridden rants, which continues to be the pattern for the next 364 days. Sometimes, insecurity looks like being controlling. Sometimes, it looks like being dominating toward and pushing away the very person you wish would wrap their arms around you and comfort you. Sometimes, it looks like being the loudest person in the room. Sometimes, it looks like being the smartest person in the room. Whatever your choice of shield, just know, things are not always what they seem; and the harder we grasp at those identities, the more we may be shielding painful and unrelenting insecurity and the lies we have come to believe about ourselves because of shame.

I did all I could to grasp at worldly forms of power and at-

tention to manage insecurity and shame: being the most pop-
ular, the loudest, the funniest, the smartest, the wisest, the ad-
vice-giver, the one who didn't need help, the one who didn't need
anyone, the one who had all the answers. In college, I was the
party girl. I remember once sitting on the floor in the closet of
my bedroom, overwhelmed because all I wanted to do was stay
home and hang out with one of my roommates for the evening,
but I had managed to say yes to multiple sets of plans and didn't
know how to simply say no to any of them, because I was afraid
to put even the slightest dent in the shield that safeguarded my
insecurity and shame.

Once I graduated from college and started working in banking, some things began to unravel. When we're in middle school
and high school, the ways we grasp at power to mask deep-seat-
ed insecurity quite frankly just look like developmentally appropriate behaviors for an adolescent. In college, when you're one of
perhaps four Black people, you can blame sticking out like a sore
thumb on your Blackness instead of a subconscious, carefully
laid plan to ensure that no one finds out how insecure you really
are. Also, just another tip: Usually most people around us will
know we struggle with insecurity, and they'll do a much better
job seeing us the way that God sees us; really, we're only fooling
ourselves. When I arrived on the corporate scene, it was a matter
of months before I was invited into a small leadership role. From
there, it was fast forward. The years 2005 to 2010 were a career
whirlwind for me. I was promoted several times. I had roles as a
team manager, an operations manager, a special projects manager, and then a larger-level project manager. I had managed a ton
of people and a ton of projects. I had found what would be my
new power source: power in my career.

I didn't sleep. I worked from 7 a.m. to sometime after mid-
night. I worked on the weekends. Once, I was hospitalized for
asthma, and I was trying to get a laptop so I could work. It was

really too easy — me, a daughter of Eve, grasping at low-hang-
ing fruit so I could say I did it my way. Yet, in the midst of it
all, I was still slowly growing in my faith. I had not stopped
being a Christian. Two years after graduating from college, in
2005, I became Catholic. I continued to go to Mass on Sundays,
confess when I needed to go to confession, jam my Gospel music in my car, have those big emotional cries at retreats as is
appropriate — and then return to my same behaviors on Mon-
day morning. There is something about being a Catholic and a
Christian; sometimes we know how to go through the motions,
but we have not really surrendered our lives to God. Instead,
we're walking in deep self-reliance and self-sufficiency, standing trapped in the garden with Adam and Eve, doubting the
goodness of our Father, tempted to grasp at a power that we
could never hold.

• • •

I have become convinced that our lives are one long surrendering,
degree by degree. We don't do it all at once, because God knows
we simply can't all at once. We
underestimate the weight of
original sin, the weight of that
faint whisper that asks, *Can I
really count on the Father? Is God
really good?* Little by little, we
walk away from the tree with
Adam and Eve, and toward the
tree of the cross, toward Jesus

> I HAVE BECOME
> CONVINCED THAT
> OUR LIVES ARE ONE
> LONG SURRENDERING,
> DEGREE BY DEGREE.

and Mary, and surrender to being transformed into the likeness
of Christ, degree by degree.

There I was, with great opportunities at the bank, great
jobs, amazing mentors who taught me skills and mindsets that

I still use today, jacked into what seemed like an unlimited power source provided courtesy of the American dream. I had returned from a trip to Rome, as I mentioned previously, and had gotten a spiritual director. In that relationship, I began to discern religious life, and that called for a therapist, because I was truly overwhelmed by it all. I chose a non-Catholic therapist, since I thought my discernment would be a key topic of discussion for us, and I didn't want a counselor who might feel pressured to encourage a vocation in me if that wasn't God's call for my life. I felt like I could count on a Protestant counselor to not do that. With my first counselor, my understanding of power began to unravel, and it continues to unravel to this day. My first counselor, Brad, was great. A light-hearted, joyful guy, a devoted father, a faith-filled man. I thought we would be talking about my discernment of religious life. As it turned out, we would spend two years talking about that and many other things. One day, Brad gave me a homework assignment for the week. He asked me over the next week until our next appointment to begin making a list of the things I can control. In my sheer ignorance, I said, "Sure!" as if someone would need a week for that assignment. Each day I started to add things to the list and then stopped my hand from writing, realizing I actually didn't have control over what I was about to write down. I was becoming distressed. It was now about five days since my last session, and I realized the whole assignment was a trick question.

Myself. All I could control was myself.

Everything else — literally, everything else — is not in my control. I was walking back from lunch one day with all this rumbling around in my mind, and I stepped onto the elevator with another woman. We hit our floor buttons and then she turned and said to me, seeming like a messenger from God with her timing, "About fifteen minutes ago, this elevator malfunctioned and dropped to the bottom floor and a man broke his leg." That right there will forever be my metaphor for the illusion of control. At any moment, the elevator could drop to the bottom floor — the elevator of your career, the elevator of your health or the health of your loved ones, the elevator of your relationships — at any moment, so much can change.

When we live our lives as if we have control beyond ourselves — our own choices and behaviors, how we spend our time in this life, and what we give the most meaning to (as though this world and our circumstances and the people in our lives are ours to control) — we render ourselves helpless and hopeless. We make the entirety of our lives — the meaning in all that is around us — only as big and able to stretch only as far as the one single breath in our nostrils. What a waste to limit the grandeur of God to the illusion of being controlled by a creature who cannot even hold more than a single breath in his or her nostrils at a time. What a waste to say the life of your child is under your command; you who can only hold a single breath in your nostrils, desire more for your child. Desire more for your aging parents. Desire more for the injustices in the world. Desire an eternal Father who breathes the breath of life through the Word His Son and Their Spirit, who goes well beyond you or me; that's what our loved ones and our lives deserve.

> *DESIRE AN ETERNAL FATHER WHO BREATHES THE BREATH OF LIFE THROUGH THE WORD HIS SON AND THEIR SPIRIT, WHO GOES WELL BEYOND YOU OR ME; THAT'S WHAT OUR LOVED ONES AND OUR LIVES DESERVE.*

• • •

When I look back at those years of scrambling around, looking for an anchor in the world, looking for some sense of security and stability in a ground that would always be shifting, the girl from the sixteenth chapter of Ezekiel comes to mind:

> As for your birth, on the day you were born your navel cord was not cut; you were not washed with water or anointed; you were not rubbed with salt or wrapped in swaddling clothes. No eye looked on you with pity or compassion to do any of these things for you. Rather, on the day you were born you were left out in the field, rejected.
>
> Then I passed by and saw you struggling in your blood, and I said to you in your blood, "Live!" I helped you grow up like a field plant, so that you grew, maturing into a woman with breasts developed and hair grown; but still you were stark naked. I passed by you again and saw that you were now old enough for love. So I spread the corner of my cloak over you to cover your nakedness; I swore an oath to you and entered into covenant with you … and you became mine. Then I bathed you with water, washed away your blood, and anointed you with oil. I clothed you with an embroidered gown, put leather sandals on your feet; I gave you a fine linen sash and silk robes to wear. I adorned you with jewelry, putting bracelets on your arms, a necklace about your neck, a ring in your nose, earrings in your ears, and a beautiful crown on your head. Thus, you were adorned with gold and silver; your garments made of fine linen, silk, and embroidered cloth. Fine flour, honey, and olive oil were your food. You were very, very beautiful, fit for

royalty. You were renowned among the nations for your
beauty, perfected by the splendor I showered on you. …
But you trusted in your own beauty. (Ezekiel 16:4–15)

The girl in this story is restored as a daughter and also as a spouse.
Yet, instead of trusting in the one who is the root, foundation,
and source of her dignity, she turns to her own strength. She will
go on to sell herself and her own children for the favor of others and for high places. She will build platforms to make herself
more available to more people to whom she can sell herself. She
becomes caught in a trap, an exhausting cycle of self-sufficiency
and striving to know a glimmer of the love that God already
offered to her abundantly and freely. She chooses the path that
allows her to feel seemingly in control, contrary to the path of
surrendered receptivity before God — a God who had perfected
her by the splendor He freely showered upon her. She, much like
Eve once did, refuses to be a recipient of an inheritance from the
Father; she refuses to let God, who is first Father, and also will
go on to establish a spousal relationship with His people, provide
her with all that she is and will be. She rejects God's fatherhood,
she rejects being His daughter, and so ultimately, she rejects the
opportunity to be His spouse.

I believe hope in the world is profoundly crippled because
we culturally struggle with the rejection of fatherhood — the
fundamental fatherhood found in the life of God. We struggle to
live as heirs, heirs of salvation, of mercy, and of even the single
breath held and suspended in our nostrils giving us the gift of
life in this very moment. We struggle with the fact that before
God, the human person can only be receptive; even what we offer back to God was first given to us by God. We struggle with
the tension and fear that arises at the idea of receiving that gift
from a God we have perhaps refused to know, or perhaps still
struggle to trust. I read an article once that was an interview with

Cardinal Robert Sarah about his book *The Day Is Far Spent*. The theme was focused on his warning to the West, and he included his ideas about our rejection of fatherhood and where this leads:

> I would like to emphasize the rejection of fatherhood. Our contemporaries are convinced that, in order to be free, one must not depend on anybody. There is a tragic error in this. Western people are convinced that receiving is contrary to the dignity of human persons. But civilized man is fundamentally an heir, he receives a history, a culture, a language, a name, a family. ... To refuse to be inscribed within a network of dependence, heritage, and filiation condemns us. ...
>
> I want to suggest to Western people that the real cause of this refusal to claim their inheritance and this refusal of fatherhood is the rejection of God. ... The West refuses to receive, and will accept only what it constructs for itself. ... This revolt is spiritual at root. It is the revolt of Satan against the gift of grace. Fundamentally, I believe that Western man refuses to be saved by God's mercy. He refuses to receive salvation, wanting to build it for himself.

We try to use self-sufficiency and the illusion that we can be the author of our whole lives to soothe the tension and pain that comes with being an heir while we are in an imperfect relationship with God. If this is you, with me you will only find compassion. I understand clenched fists before a provident God. I understand compounding old shame with new shame once you realize your fists are clenched before a *loving* God, and even though you know who He is now, for the life of you, you still cannot get your heart to open. It took me years to understand what my father's suicide meant for my view of God the Father. It took me years to start unclenching those fingers, and honestly there are times and areas of my life where I am still stuck with a death grip on some temporal reality that I am substituting for my inheritance as a child of God, for the crown He wishes to place on my head: the crown of the freedom of the children of God. It is the greatest paradox: To be free, I must bow down in surrender; to be free, I must extend my heart to hope that will speak into eternity, every second of every day.

> *IT IS THE GREATEST PARADOX: TO BE FREE I MUST BOW DOWN IN SURRENDER; TO BE FREE I MUST EXTEND MY HEART TO HOPE THAT WILL SPEAK INTO ETERNITY, EVERY SECOND OF EVERY DAY.*

Instead, we scrape and scramble and compare and compete. At the first sign of danger, we hoard as many resources as our arms can hold because we fear there will not be enough; we fear *we* will not be enough. We assume we are in the midst of scarcity, when in fact God has promised to fulfill our needs. We espouse models for healing oppression that simply assert that the way forward is to exchange dominance for dominance, oppression for oppression. On the other hand, we sit silent in the face of blatant injustice, classism, racism, discrimination, and the enduring, age-old subtleties of white supremacy, because we are afraid to lose the privileges that those dispositions afforded us while others have been held hostage in the snares of generational injustice. We take the gifts that God has given us to be eloquent with words and we exploit them, drafting lovely essays, books, sermons, and talks that craftily allow these dispositions to endure. What's worse, we cloak these dispositions in a veneer of the kingdom by throwing around words like *love*, *peace*, and *justice*, but our words are void of sacrifice and action and a true desire for reconciliation and reparation. We build the platforms of the woman in Ezekiel, selling ourselves over and over and over again to the culture. Running about in the culture, in our political parties, in our preferred media outlets, in our preferred echo chambers, running about like children who have no father, like children who have no home, like children who are not clothed by the love of God himself, like children who are not heirs to the entire kingdom of God, anointed priest, prophet, and king. Selling ourselves to whoever will look, because our hope is in our own strength and not the strength of the Lord.

This is the hope in our world, and it has crept into our Church. No, I am going to be honest: It has flooded our Church. It is what is causing our Catholic media to become so polarized. Our Catholic media outlets seem to have become self-soothing ointment for whichever side of the Catholic aisle they cater to, rather than ministries to bring people to Jesus Christ. We have religious leaders who are steeped in self-reliance, which is worldly hope, instead of in the hope of the children of God. This is what has made it possible for rampant corruption in our Church to spread. Worldly hope leaves our Church leaders speaking to us more about business models and strategic plans than prayer and Jesus. This worldly hope leads to ministries full of activity and each day becoming more and more void of prayer. This worldly hope leaves the homes of families void of prayer. We are well beyond the days when we would continue to live as if prayer was reserved only for the insides of monasteries and convents. This was never the plan for prayer. We are in the days when the insides of the homes of families must be places of prayer. This worldly hope affects convents, too, as religious sisters sacrifice prayer for ministry (which is an oxymoron in a sense, because the ministry is an effect of prayer). This worldly hope, a hope that says, "I can construct my world and myself," puts us at war with our neighbors, with ourselves, and with God.

The first step beyond worldly hope is honesty. We play with so many things, filling them up with words and complexities, when in fact there is an abiding simplicity. Have we been honest about racism, or have we put one another in a double bind where the only option is failure, and reconciliation is not the goal but rather various forms of domination? Are we honest about scandal in our Church, or do we sidestep and use many words for matters that really only need a few? Do we preoccupy ourselves with the splinter in our brother's eye without being honest about and preoccupied with the plank in our own eye? Can I be honest about the world, about the Church, about myself? And slow down, friend, before you take this as an invitation to storm the internet with tough truth, as many now love to do; in many cases, they are also lying to themselves. Honesty and vulnerability are real close friends.

THE FIRST STEP BEYOND WORLDLY HOPE IS HONESTY.

So, cruel truth cloaked in orthodoxy and void of charity is not honesty. The only reason I can say all this is because I have participated in it in every way. Recently, God revealed to me a way that I had been refusing to receive from Him as an heir. He also revealed my heart to me and how scared and prideful and hurt I was. Through the tears, I found myself repeatedly apologizing to God, saying over and over again, "I am sorry." I know about self-sufficiency. I know about worldly hope. I know how hard it is to put down that dang apple, be honest with myself, and walk out of the Garden to the cross. I know how hard it is to figure out what that looks like in daily life, because sometimes it means speaking up, and sometimes it means shutting up. Sometimes, it means taking an action, and sometimes it means being still. Sometimes, it's saying yes, and sometimes it's saying no. Sometimes, it's realizing that the world is not going to collapse if I take a day off, or if I take a leave of absence for my family or for my health — because the world does not in fact hope in the one breath held in my nostrils.

Through baptism we are anointed as priest, prophet, and king. By the gift of this sacrament and the sacramental graces, we have the privilege of sitting on the throne of hope. When we give in to worldly hope, we abdicate this throne; we abdicate our power. See, I actually think it's OK to want power. I think it's OK to look for a shield for that abiding insecurity we probably won't fully shake until we see God face to face. We just need something bigger than the one breath we're holding in our nostrils! When it's based on us, we will only be left grasping and grappling. We need a hope that extends well beyond ourselves and into eternity; a hope that comes from a God who not only has given us hope, but allows us to spread this hope to others on His behalf. We simply need to take our seats on this freely given throne that has been prepared for us; this is our power. "The virtue of hope responds to the aspiration to happiness which God has placed in the heart of every man" (CCC 1818). So, you see, nothing else was ever going to do because even that restlessness and aspiration, that longing, is also a part of our inheritance.

BY THE GIFT OF BAPTISM AND THE SACRAMENTAL GRACES, WE HAVE THE PRIVILEGE OF SITTING ON THE THRONE OF HOPE.

3

DISCERNMENT: SCHOOL OF HOPE

Closer is He than breathing.

— *Alfred Lord Tennyson*

If God is the giver of the gift of even the breath I just drew, then His presence is not only constant, it is quite intimate. As we slowly surrender hope that is of the world (a self-reliant hope that relies solely on the extent of human power), we have the option to embrace something more. This is a process, much like surrendering worldly hope is a process. Discernment has an acute ability to take us to school in this effort, but from my experience this occurs in stages. First, we learn to discern between good and evil. Next, we learn the art of discerning between two goods, which is where most people will stop their journey in the art of discernment. This is the type of discernment we use when discerning our vocation. But there is a third type of discernment: a seeking for the transcendent, faith dimension in the midst of our ordinary, everyday experiences. To put it more simply, this third type of discernment involves discerning the gift of the nearness that God has to us; this is a lifelong task.

In order to share with you my own experiences of discernment, I need to backtrack a little to what brought me to the University of Dallas to study for my undergraduate degree. It was simple, really. I was an eighteen-year-old girl, making some of my very first efforts at grown-up discernment. I knew it would not be good for me to be too far away from home (so stay in Texas). I knew that I needed to feel a part of a community (a small school), and that I wanted to be around nice people (the folks from UD seemed nice enough!). So, I enrolled at the University of Dallas without realizing it was Catholic! To be fair, I do not know if it would have made much difference to me if someone had clearly laid out for me what a Catholic identity meant for a school. I was not formed enough to understand the meaning of any of that. The disposition of the folks at the school was a much clearer testimony to me as a young girl than lofty speeches about a profound Catholic identity would ever have been.

THIS THIRD TYPE OF DISCERNMENT INVOLVES DISCERNING THE GIFT OF THE NEARNESS THAT GOD HAS TO US; THIS IS A LIFELONG TASK.

To be honest, I grappled a lot with discernment between good and evil while I was in college, and this was most pronounced during my semester in Rome as a sophomore student.

We all live with one foot in the world and one in eternity, awaiting the redemption of our bodies, while an immortal soul animates each of us, and my semester in Rome made this reality very stark for me. One night I would be partying and making the unwise decisions that can sometimes be characteristic of a college student, and the very next day I was falling in love with the Catholic Church. The best way to put what was going on between the Church and me, I think, is that I was intoxicated with the Catholic Faith; my senses were completely filled up with the sounds, the smells, the sights, the beauty, the reverence; this increased my own longing to taste and see the goodness of the Lord (see Ps 34:9). I loved Pope St. John Paul II (who was still pope at that time). As a Baptist college student, I thought he was simply a phenomenal preacher. I did not know anything about popes. I had no idea what was going on in the liturgy. But I knew beauty, and I knew John Paul II was talking to me about the God I had grown up getting to know, and he was taking me deeper.

I was sheltered from the drama of the Catholic right versus the Catholic left, which I am convinced is a well-laid plan of satan. Imagine the strategy of the evil one: With this division we nurture in our Church between what we have coined "the left" and "the right," the "liberal" and the "conservative," we are left with two choices. Either we are navel-gazing, running to echo chambers full of those who think just like us and are self-proclaimed warriors, martyrs, and victims, courageously fighting against the other "side." Or option two, we spend our time finger-pointing, developing whole media platforms and ministries aimed at pointing out what is wrong with those on the wrong side of the Church. With an ongoing preoccupation with these two all-too-often chosen dispositions, we manage to spend less and less time actually focused on Jesus and on feeding His sheep and serving the coming of the kingdom. As a college student in Rome, none of this was on my radar; I was simply intoxicated by the beauty, awakened by the preaching of the word, inspired by the reverence and devotion of other worshipers, and challenged by the pursuit of virtue in those around me.

When I returned from Rome, I joined a polyphonic Latin liturgical choir that was coordinated through the university. As it turned out, I was catechized and evangelized in that choir. We sang countless Masses. I learned the Mass parts through what we sang. I learned about the mystery of purgatory by singing Gabriel Fauré's *Requiem*. I learned the gift of the Triduum by serving in music ministry with this choir, singing through the sacred days of Holy Thursday, Good Friday, and Holy Saturday. The only word for this experience — this movement that drew my heart away from the first stage of discernment (grappling with choosing between good and evil) to a steadier focus on discernment between varying goods — is *romance*. This was a romance. My godfather told me once that the way the word *romance* as seen by many today has lost some of its original meaning and beauty. He taught me that originally, *romance* referenced the adventures of a hero. In that sense, true discernment is a romance, an adventure with God and with His Church; Jesus is the hero.

Still, I had the firm intention to not become Catholic, for one abiding reason. Church as a Baptist woman was the only place I went where I was not one of few or no other Black people present. At school there were few Black people, at Catholic Masses there were few to no Black people. Most of the places I went, there were not people who looked like me. If I was no longer Baptist, then I would lose the one place at that time in my life where I went and was not the minority.

All of us who are Catholic have to face and resolve the fact that Black Americans have not been intentionally sought out and invited to the Eucharistic table. From the very beginning of our Church, the apostles did not sit in Jerusalem saying, "Anyone who can make it over here to where we are is welcome to join us."

They went out. The fruit of their love for Jesus literally launched them forth into the world to make disciples of all nations. Parthia, Asia Minor, Africa, Antioch, and so many more. I had come to the University of Dallas, this place where the Eucharistic Lord dwelled, and I could encounter Him. I long for the day when that same Lord, inflamed in the hearts of believers, enters into parts of our dioceses where we have either been afraid or been forgetful to go. It overwhelms me now to think that I might not have found my faith and my vocation if I had not been willing to enter this Catholic world; that it is likely that no one would have left that Catholic world to come looking for me — a child of God clearly called to the Eucharistic table. I cried when I realized that my desire for the Eucharist had superseded my desire to hold onto the gift and fullness of the Black experience in the Baptist Church. These tears were tears of grief.

There is a little grief in discernment; first we say goodbye to evils that we have made our comforts in order to choose good. Then it gets a little harder. We surrender some goods to pursue other goods. I departed from an experience of faith where my Blackness was celebrated and upheld (a good) into an experience of faith where my Blackness was barely mentioned, and certainly rarely celebrated as a gift (not a good), and I would have to put forth personal effort for the gift of Blackness to be celebrated. I made this choice for the Eucharist (the supreme good).

I wonder if many of us pause here in the school of discernment because of the cost and the pain, and don't venture on. The pain of saying no to marriage to say yes to the priesthood or religious life. The pain of saying no to the priesthood or religious life to say yes to marriage. The pain of saying no to my personal preferences (at least to a certain degree) for the sake of the common good. The pain of departing from an experience of faith from childhood that comforted and affirmed me, to venture out in faith that I might taste and see the goodness of the Eucharistic Lord. To discern means to judge well. When we judge well, we make decisions, recognizing that to have one thing means I cannot have all the things, even if they are all good. I think this is one of the struggles in our world. We avoid the pain of choosing and committing to one choice, so instead we grasp at all the options.

TO DISCERN MEANS TO JUDGE WELL.

I remember once I had the honor of a woman asking me to accompany her spiritually. She was in what she called an open marriage. I mean it when I say it was an honor; she was an incredibly beautiful person in many ways, and she was also dealing with significant vulnerabilities. I was not able to accompany her at that time in my own journey, and I certainly had to be honest with her about my hope for her sacramental marriage, and I will never forget her. All that she wanted was good. She sought love as she understood it. Nothing that she grasped at was intrinsically evil; ultimately, hers was an avoidance of the pain of choice and of the task to grieve what goods we surrender to pursue the good we are called to. Like so many of us, she did not want to decide. The word *decide* at its root references the Latin verb meaning "to slay" or "to cut off," similar to incision. I used to crack jokes about the tearful and overwhelmed women who would approach me in vocations ministry and admit for the first time that they want to discern religious life because they think God might be calling them to be a religious sister or consecrated woman. Nine out of ten times before they could finish what they planned to say, they had begun to cry, hard. I no longer think this is a laughing matter. I think these women are acutely aware of our call to cut off or to slay so that we might choose and judge well. We have the duty and the right to mourn what we have cut off, especially if it was good.

The counselor in me, and also the part of me who has had to cut away things that were once useful but are now no longer useful, needs to add something here in case it might be helpful to you. There may have been points in our lives where we were surviving hardships, abuse, addiction, trauma, or any suffering where we developed habits and patterns that helped us to survive. Those patterns and habits were useful and served a good *when they were useful and served a good*. At some point, in many cases, they became no longer useful to us. Perhaps your patterns and habits included isolation, overeating, perfectionism, conflict avoidance, people-pleasing, manipulation, control — this list could get long. Although for a time the habit served a purpose, in most cases, it eventually ceases to be useful, and often it becomes harmful. I know it is hard to cut these away. I know as a counselor, and I know from personal experience. So, I just want to say, if it takes you some time to put them down, that's OK. You can put them down when you are ready.

Can you see it now? How this process of discernment is a school of hope? Why do we bother to discern good over evil? Why choose a God we cannot see and the good of a soul within ourselves that we cannot touch when evil so often brings immediate pleasure and gratification, whether it's sexual sin, excessive drinking, drugs, love of money, or greed? Why would anyone take the time to commit and devote themselves to one good over other goods? I choose this one man to be my spouse, saying no to all other men. I choose this one woman as my spouse, saying no to all other women. I choose Jesus as my spouse, saying no to sacramental marriage. I choose the Church as my bride, as a priest, saying no to sacramental marriage. I choose to not commit this mortal sin so that I might not separate myself from Jesus, the Church, and the Eucharistic table. For what and for whom would I make such a sacrifice? Saint Paul reminds us: "For in hope we were saved. Now hope that sees for itself is not hope. For who hopes for what one sees? But if we hope for what we do not see, we wait with endurance" (Rom 8:24–25). Slowly but surely, with the help of the Eucharist, we cut away what each of us must as we grow in hope for what we do not see: Christ himself and the fullness of His kingdom. How do we come to know what we do not see? What draws us into this willingness to ultimately sacrifice all for that which we have not yet seen? This is the last class in the school of discernment, the search for the transcendent faith dimension in the midst of our ordinary experiences, where we glimpse or see a glimmer of what is hoped for.

I know that there are so many influences that encourage us to consider discernment as a matter related to determining which vocation God has called each one of us to. But in my opinion, that is far too limiting. Discernment is a key part of this romance between you and God and His people and His Church. I think we need to talk less about discerning our vocations and talk more about discerning the enduring presence of God in every aspect of our lives — the abiding and loving providence of the Lord that gives us confidence to face whatever may be before us, because He is with us always, even until the end of the age (see Mt 28:20). He is our sure hope. I think we need to talk more about learning how to pray so that we might look on the world with this kingdom vision, having the capacity to look all around us and discern the presence of the kingdom.

I used to have something all backwards. I would tell people that when we were dwelling in the past or preoccupied with the future, we had fallen into the trap of trying to be like God. I was wrong. When we dwell in the past or preoccupy ourselves with the future, we have departed from the great gift bestowed upon us to be like God; we only encounter God in the present moment. When we discern the length, width, height, and depth of

God's love (see Eph 3:18) that permeates each present moment of our lives, and can find it in ourselves to respond to this love with love (willing the good), then we are like God. This is not easy, and it can be an overwhelming task.

When I was in RCIA and it came time to pick a confirmation saint, it took me a while to land on which saint God was clearly calling me to all along, solely due to my stubbornness. I wanted a fancy saint, someone nobody knew, so I could be constantly educating people about my special saint. Yet, throughout my shenanigans, it was clear that God was revealing Saint Cecilia to me. Music has been a key part of my journey to the Faith, both as a child, and later in college, and the call to choose Saint Cecilia was connected to that. I eventually listened and chose Saint Cecilia. We had to write an essay about our choice, and I took the opportunity to share about my very first solo that I sang as a child at Central Garden Missionary Baptist Church. It was an important moment in my life, discovering worship through music, discovering that my own voice was able to lift up this praise. It was a Gospel song that I wrote about. The morning I walked into RCIA to turn in my essay, our director (also a Black American woman, which had been a beautiful consolation from the Lord to me) was playing on the stereo the very song she had no idea I had written about. I remember being overwhelmed by the almost absurd coincidence. Walking

WHEN WE DWELL IN THE PAST OR PREOCCUPY OURSELVES WITH THE FUTURE, WE HAVE DEPARTED FROM THE GREAT GIFT BESTOWED UPON US TO BE LIKE GOD; WE ONLY ENCOUNTER GOD IN THE PRESENT MOMENT.

into my RCIA class at a predominantly white Catholic parish and my Black American RCIA director playing the Gospel song that was my first solo as a child growing up and also the subject of the essay I was holding in my hand — I turned around and walked out. It was too much nearness. I called a friend, and she said such wise words to me. She told me it can be overwhelming how concerned God is for us, it can be scary. What will we do with this love? How on earth could we ever respond to this love?

One of my religious sisters who studies Hebrew shared with me once that the Scripture that describes each of us as the apple of God's eye is not the best translation. She told me that the better translation is "the little man in God's eye." God's eye is so fixed on you that you become a reflection in His eye. We were promised Emmanuel — God with us. God with us in every detail: "Before I formed you in the womb I knew you" (Jer 1:5); "You know when I sit and stand" (Ps 139:2); "You will not abandon my soul" (Ps 16:10); "You will show me the path to life" (Ps 16:11). What would marriages, the priesthood, and the state of religious life look like if we had a world full of people seeking to discern the enduring love of God that permeates the simple and ordinary experiences of our lives? Discern that. Act from that. Decide from that. It will make you a warrior of hope. You will see the kingdom here, and at the same time await it, in labor pains. Discern the "loving press" of God, as Bishop Robert Barron says, without which we could not continue to exist.

What does this look like in daily life? How does discernment become a school of hope?

It looks like deciding to get help with your pornography addiction because you have chosen to walk the path of putting down pornography for pursuit of the good — because you have hope that the good will in fact lead you to the kingdom as God has promised.

It looks like doing more listening than talking in your marriage and taking a chance on your spouse in that part of your marriage where you have been overly dominant, controlling, or domineering. It looks like being the first to apologize because both of you are wrong, and not revoking your apology if you do not hear what you want to hear after you have made it. You hope that cleaning up your side of the street, and making that first apology, surrendering the outcome, will bear fruit in the relationship.

It looks like knowing that coincidences are God's providence, and pausing and giving praise and thanks to God for His involvement in your life.

It looks like gazing out at the soccer field as your friend, who used to be a complete hot mess in college, walks out onto it to comfort his small son as his son begins his very first game, and seeing in almost a flash what God has done with that hot mess of a college kid, now a man and a father, that most people thought would not become much, and letting yourself shed a few tears of gratitude at the privilege of knowing someone long enough to be able to spot those miracles.

> *IN THIS SCHOOL OF DISCERNMENT, AS YOU SURRENDER WORLDLY HOPE AND A FALSE FILLED CUP, THE PROBLEM OF HOPE WILL PRESENT ITSELF.*

It looks like seeing the brokenness in our institutional Church and not giving up, seeing where God is still working miracles and abiding in our mess, just like He chose to abide in the mess of a stable.

It looks like walking across that threshold of a convent door for the first time in response to a call you believe may be coming from God to religious life.

It looks like walking away from that relationship that you want to hold on to, but you know is taking you further away from the kingdom.

It looks like deciding, over and over again for the kingdom you await, and also for the kingdom that is in a way already here, nearer than breath. In this school of discernment, as you surrender worldly hope and a false-filled cup, the problem of hope will present itself. As you see more of the kingdom, you will hope for more of the kingdom, and your longing will increase as you learn more and more what is not yet, but longed for — and assured.

4

COMMUNITY: WHERE ETERNAL HOPE IS BORN IN THE WORLD

Indeed, the Lord Jesus, when He prayed to the Father, "that all may be one ... as we are one" (Jn 17:21–22) opened up vistas closed to human reason, for He implied a certain likeness between the union of the divine Persons, and the unity of God's sons in truth and charity. This likeness reveals that man, who is the only creature on earth which God willed for itself, cannot fully find himself except through a sincere gift of himself.

— Gaudium et Spes, *24*

Relationships are a crucible. A crucible is a place where different elements interact, sometimes under severe trial, to make something new. So, indeed, our relationships are crucibles! The question is, what is the new thing that is made? We will come back to that later. During the time I spent considering religious life, I was also studying Pope St. John Paul II's theology of the body for the first time. I had the privilege of studying the work of this great pope with friends once a week in a study group setting; it was the perfect way to take in this deep and profound work. During those Wednesday night groups, I learned about the sacramentality of relationships. During those weekly meetings with peers and friends, I learned that the human person is a gift, who is only ever properly received as a gift and should never be used. I learned that the opposite of love is not hate, it is actually use: to use another person for my own sake. I learned that apart from relationships in which we can live out the dimension of ourselves as gift, we cannot understand ourselves, and this is how we image God.

APART FROM RELATIONSHIPS IN WHICH WE CAN LIVE OUT THE DIMENSION OF OURSELVES AS GIFT, WE CANNOT UNDERSTAND OURSELVES, AND THIS IS HOW WE IMAGE GOD.

As God is a communion of persons, Father, Son, and Holy Spirit, so are we called to live in communion, and we only make sense in communion. As a result of those Wednesday meetings, my study group would often say things to each other like, "You are a gift." We would take this attitude into our daily lives, asking ourselves, "How am I called to be a gift in this situation?" or "How am I called to make a gift of myself in this situation?" It really was, as the Second Vatican Council document *Gaudi-*

um et Spes (On the Church in the Modern World) describes it, a whole new vista opened up for me. It resonated with me because relationships had always been important to me and a source of profound meaning in my life. I could look at the relationship between my aunt and uncle and their perseverance in their marriage and know something about how we are all called to love. I had been loved, protected, and cared for by my older brothers, and that taught me something about myself and my dignity. I had formed friendships in school and church that were more like sibling and familial bonds, and that was a whisper of what I would come to understand more clearly in religious life. I had found incredibly meaningful relationships in college — people who would become lifelong friends and give me the honor of having a front-row seat in their lives, which is really a front-row seat to watching the work of God unfold in each one of them. And they returned that gift to me, being present to me in a lifelong way. When I became Catholic, I continued to find the most beautiful and meaningful relationships, which provided me a place to flourish. Yet, before entering religious life, I do not know that I would have called relationships a crucible. Before entering religious life, I didn't yet have a firm grasp on the spiritual dimensions of relationships.

I love when people ask me the question, "How did you know?" regarding my decision to answer what I believe to be God's call to religious life. The answer is that I did not know! I had no idea how it was all going to turn out. For me, it was a totally step-by-step situation. At the first step (candidacy), the call was not to make perpetual vows, it was simply a call to be a candidate. Then, it was a call to be a postulant; and it was not until the novitiate that I firmly resolved, I am called to be Jesus' spouse, and it is the desire of my own heart to say yes. I was good with it being a step-by-step process. I was not one of those women who gets that distant look in her eyes, as though she's gazing off into a faraway, mystical place, one hand placed over her heart, whispering in a light, higher-pitched-than-her-natural voice, "God has called me to be His spouse." I was more like this: "See what had happened was that somewhere along the way I just really started to love God. I don't even really get it, and I feel a little crazy even saying that out loud, but I also don't mind sounding crazy, because I really love God, and I finally get and understand what He has done and is doing for me, and I cannot stand the thought of refusing to love Him back by not seeing what this religious life business that He has clearly impressed on my heart and mind is all about. So I don't know, I just know I feel like it will harm our relationship and break Jesus' heart if I intentionally refuse to do the best I can to take Him at His word, and I am realizing that He has a real heart, and I am trying to break His heart less often these days." Far less eloquent, I know, but that's more what it looked like for me.

So, I went barreling into religious life with very little expectation, and I know now that this was a grace. After about two years of visiting the convent for weekend stays four times a year, I entered formation (or moved in) as a candidate, or what we call an affiliate, in November 2011. I was, of course, shocked by the call to discern religious life. I was working in banking, getting promoted in my career, I didn't know any sisters, and I did not know anything about religious life. I had made new friends through my theology of the body study group, and one of them was discerning religious life and asked me to be her "wingman" on her next planned discernment retreat weekend. That discernment weekend was planned with the Sisters of the Holy Family of Nazareth, who would become my sisters — and I would become that friend's maid of honor! My spiritual director at that time, Father Jonathan, encouraged me to understand two things: one, that if God was calling me to be a sister, I would not be a sister overnight, so I could settle down with the panic; and two, that my main objective was to simply get to know some sisters. The wingman invitation came on the heels of Father Jonathan's guidance; the providence of it all could not be ignored. Slowly, over two years of visiting, I began to be able to see myself more and more in life as a sister, and the desire to go forward only strengthened, and so did the graces. When I became an affiliate, I was a vice president in Bank of America's home loans division. I had managed a staff of over 200, many of whom I truly came to love (they would tell you it was tough love!). I had served as a project manager on large-scale projects for our department, and I was formed by mentors who taught me how to be a leader and gave me invaluable skills. I was working for our senior vice president, working from home (a.k.a., working from the convent). I was vice president by day and baby-nun-in-the-making by night. And so, the crucible began.

It is a crucible of joy, life in community; at the very end of the day, it is always joy. There are conflicts, and then joy; there are tears, and then joy; there is hard work, and then joy; there is struggle and joy; sickness, infirmity, death, and joy. The abiding theme for me has been joy. Early on in my affiliate, I began to reflect on what was going on in the relationships among the sisters. I was scandalized by the ordinariness of it all. I was scandalized by the troubles that seemed misplaced among women who clearly loved Jesus so much. I had embraced the accusation that those who have espoused themselves to secular culture love to make about Christians as a way to excuse themselves for their own childish refusal to believe in anything that might cost them anything. I was asking myself, how could women who say they love Jesus so much have conflicts and struggles and argue and give each other the silent treatment, and so on? I was judgmental. One day I decided to take my judgments to a couple of sisters, and in summary, this is what I walked away with (I will never forget it): I was challenged to look at religious life with a different lens. I was challenged to recognize that our convents were not a collection of women who had had the privilege and comfort of hand-picking who they would live with (like one big, lifelong, dorm slumber party), but who had rather received the sisters with whom they lived from God as expressed in the authority of the congregation. I was challenged to look on our homes and see the miracle of it all: that women who did not hand-pick each other, and had come from such different backgrounds and families, were now gathered around the Eucharist, striving each day not only for personal holiness, but communal holiness. Women whom the world would never have labeled as making sense together, by virtue of a love of Jesus that bore fruit in a consecration to Him through the holy vows, were now actually family. Family, not in spite of our struggles, but through the crucible of our struggles.

EACH VOW TEACHES US SOMETHING ABOUT RIGHT RELATIONSHIP AND SERVES AS A PROPHECY ABOUT THE TYPES OF RELATIONSHIPS EVERYONE IS CALLED TO, NOT JUST RELIGIOUS SISTERS, BROTHERS, AND PRIESTS.

It's been said to me often that because of the structure of religious life, who I live with will always be changing, and this will make my life hard. But aren't we all dealing with one version or another of hard? How on earth would we grow if we weren't? I was challenged by my sisters to see the miracle that women who, according to the standards of the world, should have been strangers, now lived together, prayed together, shared meals together, learned to love one another, and learned to bear with and forgive one another, and that this was good news, and a sign that Christ has indeed come. The vows had disposed the sisters to receive these graces, because the vows are a vehicle for right relationship. Each vow teaches us something about right relationship and serves as a prophecy about the types of relationships everyone is called to, not just religious sisters, brothers, and priests.

Poverty is about right relationship with the providence of God. We often stunt a mature understanding of the vow of poverty by the oversimplification that if I have nothing, then I am living poverty. I remember once a woman was holding my Apple phone for me and said, "Religious life surely pays off!" To which I responded, "One hundredfold in fact." The only-focused-on-having-nothing approach to poverty is a bit of a missed mark. Saint Paul alludes to the heart of the matter when he writes that he is able to live well both in abundance and in humble circumstances, because he has learned the secret (see Phil 4:12). The secret is in the example of the Old Testament *anawim*. *Anawim* is a Hebrew word that in Scripture refers to the poor ones of God. They were not a group to feel sorry for; however, they were a group whose lead was worth following. They were the poor ones of God not because of destitution, but rather because they were acutely aware that before God all is gift, even the breath that was just drawn. They embraced this blessed existential poverty as a means to welcome the love and providence of God into their hearts and souls. This spiritual poverty was an emptying out of self-sufficiency to receive all from God. Jesus was poor, for "he emptied himself, taking the form of a slave" (Phil 2:7). This was the secret that left them no longer enslaved to things of the world, or status, or praise, or the positive opinions of others. This secret allowed them to abide peacefully both in abundance (without grasping) and in humble circumstances (without fear), because they had the greatest treasure, dwelling right there inside of them as the fruit of their spiritual poverty: They were in right relationship with the providence of God — a right relationship that we are all called to, and which is prophesied through the religious vows.

Obedience is about right relationship with the will of God. The word obedience is rooted in the Latin word *oboedire*, to listen attentively or to hear. Obedience is a listening so deep that it is animated in the will. So often we refer to Mary's fiat, her assent to become the Mother of God, as a yes. But this is an impoverished translation in my opinion, because a yes is just a matter of spoken word, but her obedience was not simply spoken, it was enfleshed due to a deep animation of the will. For religious sisters, we vow obedience to the members of our congregation who have been entrusted with roles of authority and therefore are also recipients of the graces for their offices. This obedience is not about the imperfect woman before us, but more about seeking the will of God at work in her, listening deeply for this will, trusting this will, and submitting ourselves to what we have heard, so much so that our hearing is animated in our actions. It is hardly blind. The more it is perfected, the more it in fact sees; it sees the one it seeks to be united with, it sees the Heart of Jesus, perfectly aligned to the will of the Father, and it consoles that Heart through acts of obedience. I remember early on in my formation to be a religious sister, one of my brothers, who had questions, concerns, and doubts about my vocation, said to me, "Well, you know you will not be able to do what you want." I turned and looked at my uncle, who had been married to my aunt now for decades, and asked him how often he was able to "do what he wanted." His eyes sort of glazed over as he looked back into what I think had to be a time well in the past! This vow again is a prophecy made to all people by those who take it, about a reality we are all called to. We are all called to live obedience in some way. None of us has no rules to follow, none of us simply does what we want when we want, especially if we have professed to be followers of Jesus. Obedience is not exclusive to religious sisters, and it is also a foundational part of right relationship.

Lastly, our vow of chastity. I remember once a very hopeful-looking, young adult woman asked me with delight in her eyes what living the vow of chastity was like. Without thinking, I responded with one word: wild. When I saw the look of horror that crossed her sweet young face, I quickly asked her to let me explain! For those who profess the evangelical counsels of poverty, chastity, and obedience, this vow of chastity is best described as celibacy. It is one of the crowning features of religious life in the power of its prophecy, in my opinion (the other being the common life). The right relationship that celibacy offers us is right relationship with one another. Through a life of celibacy, I take no one person as my own, and no one takes me as their own. What this means is that I belong exclusively to no one, which sets me free to belong to all. Celibacy is not a turning away from the people of God; it is an unleashing of the heart for the people of God in a way of relating that is full of truth, integrity, and sincerity, absent of guile, and desiring the good. The signs and symbols of religious life cue even the most pagan and irreligious people to this wild belonging. When they see a religious, they do not see a stranger, they see someone who can enter into their lives in a meaningful way for a moment, without holding on to them, and without them feeling the need to hold on to us. We are all called to this radical and wild right relationship of belonging to one another. For now, this is lived in the Eucharist, but it will be fulfilled perfectly in eternity. A life of celibacy proclaims this hoped-for family of God in eternity.

> *CELIBACY IS NOT A TURNING AWAY FROM THE PEOPLE OF GOD; IT IS AN UNLEASHING OF THE HEART FOR THE PEOPLE OF GOD.*

***

These vows and these sisters have tuned me into the power of right relationship — the right relationship revealed in the vows. They have also made me sharply sensitive to situations that are poorly ordered toward right relationship. As time went on, I found myself growing in thirst for integrity and sincerity in settings that seemed to lack it. I recall once learning of a chaplain who served students and families who were dear to me. I would often hear feedback of blurred boundaries and misguided ways of relating between this chaplain and the students. Time and time again I spoke to people I thought were responsible for him, but I never directly spoke to him. When I finally decided to do a better job myself living in right relationship and go directly to him with my concerns, it was a revelation of truth. That's the power of right relationship: It's revelation that sets us free. In this case, the revelation was a hard truth. This young priest wasn't particularly interested in clear boundaries and right relationship. While it was not the outcome I had hoped for, by choosing integrity (going directly to him), I now had a clearer vision of the truth of the matter. Each morning in all eleven countries where Sisters of the Holy Family of Nazareth reside, we say the same prayer to the Holy Family.

WORLDLY LOVES CAUSE US TO SEEK OURSELVES. THE LOVE OF GOD HAS US SEEK THE GOOD OF THE OTHER.

The fourth part of the prayer reads, "Jesus, Mary, Joseph, inspire us so to live our community life, that we may be a sign to others that Christ has come, that our hope is centered in Him, and that we look forward to the glory of the Resurrection." Jesus, Mary, Joseph … inspire us. What do we want them to inspire us with? With their example of the kingdom of God's love, that becomes evident or manifest in the presence of right relationship. Right there in the life of the Holy Family, the love in the life of the Trinity — between the Father and the Son and the Holy Spirit — is revealed to us, in the flesh. We can take this as a model to follow and be inspired to cultivate relationships in our world that look ever more like the relationships among the Holy Family, therefore quite literally spreading God's Trinitarian love in the world, or putting flesh on God's love in the world, or, as one of my sisters likes to say, incarnate love. This is not the watered-down wasteland of love that the world presents to us. Worldly loves cause us to seek ourselves. The love of God has us seek the good of the other.

The love of God is simply sacrificial love, where I will the good of the other person. It is manifest only in deed, not in our feelings or emotions, not in words that lack action. It was right in the middle of the messiness of religious life that I discovered it. In the simplest and most ordinary of moments, when a dishwasher was emptied by one sister even though it wasn't her turn, as I walked down the hallway and saw one sister feeding another who was infirm, slowly and attentively spoonful by spoonful, as I saw sisters sit at the bedside of a dying sister, praying with her through the night so that she would die in the company of family and in the midst of prayer, as I saw a bunch of sisters pile into one car to go out for putt-putt golf even though they were all tired, because there was a need to be more intentional about building relationships in community, as I saw sisters leave ministries that perfectly delighted their hearts to serve their sisters in leadership positions that would take them to the brink of stress and hardship, as I saw sisters who had concluded a recent conflict agreeing to never speak to one another again slowly begin again to work to restore their relationship, right in front of me — hope was being born in the world, the hope of God.

The *Catechism* beautifully describes this as the hope of a new heaven and a new earth:

At the end of time, the Kingdom of God will come in its fullness. After the universal judgment, the righteous will reign for ever with Christ, glorified in body and soul. The universe itself will be renewed:

> The Church … will receive her perfection only in the glory of heaven, when will come the time of the renewal of all things. At that time, together with the human race, the universe itself, which is so closely related to man and which attains its destiny through him, will be perfectly re-established in Christ.

Sacred Scripture calls this mysterious renewal, which will transform humanity and the world, "new heavens and a new earth." It will be the definitive realization of God's plan to bring under a single head "all things in [Christ], things in heaven and things on earth."

In this new universe, the heavenly Jerusalem, God will have his dwelling among men. "He will wipe away every tear from their eyes, and death shall be no more, neither shall there be mourning nor crying nor pain any more, for the former things have passed away."

For man, this consummation will be the final realization of the unity of the human race, which God willed from creation and of which the pilgrim Church has been "in the nature of sacrament." Those who are united with Christ will form the community of the redeemed, "the holy city" of God, "the Bride, the wife of the Lamb." She will not be wounded any longer by sin, stains, self-love, that destroy or wound the earthly community. The beatific vision, in which God opens himself in an inexhaustible way to the elect, will be the ever-flowing wellspring of happiness, peace, and mutual communion.

For the cosmos, Revelation affirms the profound common destiny of the material world and man:

> For the creation waits with eager longing for the revealing of the sons of God ... in hope because the creation itself will be set free from its bondage to decay. ... We know that the whole creation has been groaning in travail together until now; and not only the creation, but we ourselves, who have the first fruits of the Spirit, groan inwardly as we wait for adoption as sons, the redemption of our bodies.

The visible universe, then, is itself destined to be transformed, "so that the world itself, restored to its original state, facing no further obstacles, should be at the service of the just," sharing their glorification in the risen Jesus Christ. (1042–1047)

The hope of God is a family, in right relationship with one another and with the world we abide in. This is unfolding, not in extravagant, titanic ways, but in the midst of ordinary life, in ordinary moments where ordinary people choose reconciliation over division, dialogue over echo chambers, sacrifice over selfishness. What

THE HOPE OF GOD IS A FAMILY, IN RIGHT RELATIONSHIP WITH ONE ANOTHER AND WITH THE WORLD WE ABIDE IN.

I think we sometimes miss is the fact that when we do this, when we take intentional steps in our daily lives to build God's family through reconciliation and sacrificial love, Christ is quite literally born in us and in the world. In the crucible of relationships, what is new that is made is the new heaven and new earth that we hope for, degree by degree, until the kingdom of God comes in its fullness, and all bears the likeness of Christ.

5

THE SAINTS: WITNESSES OF HOPE

The saints are not perfect models, but people through whom God has passed. We can compare them to the Church windows which allow light to enter in different shades of color. The saints are our brothers and sisters who have welcomed the light of God in their heart and have passed it on to the world, each according to his or her own "hue." ... This is life's purpose: to enable God's light to pass through.

— *Pope Francis*

The beautiful and simultaneously hard part about the coming of the kingdom we often hear so much about is that it is here, and at the same time, it is not. This is why Saint Paul says, "We also groan within ourselves as we wait for adoption, the redemption of our bodies" (Rom 8:23), because we have a taste of what we long for, otherwise there would be no longing, no desire for more, no striving for holiness. Because we have a foretaste, in this way, the kingdom of God is manifest to us, and also at the same time still being fulfilled.

I never had an issue delighting in the saints, and when it was time for me to engage the lives of the saints so I could choose a confirmation saint during RCIA, I was all in. As I shared earlier, I researched and researched, hoping to find a glamorous saint that no one knew about, ultimately to land on Saint Cecilia because of the gift that music had been to me in my faith journey. The essay that I walked into RCIA holding that Sunday morning told the journey of faith I had taken from being a Baptist girl to entering the Catholic Church, and how that had been a journey wrapped in music and song. Some of my most meaningful experiences with God, while I was growing up in church, took place while I was singing. As I wrote that essay, I remembered my very first solo with the youth choir. I didn't even realize I could sing like that! My godfather helped me practice, and I remember singing that song with my entire self. I was a girl who normally would have been apprehensive and self-conscious, but while praising God in music, I was anything but. Remarks after were centered on the freedom I had in worshiping God while singing. That would go on to be the case as I jumped into singing in as many youth choirs as time would allow. My godsisters and I went from practice to practice, concert to concert, worship event to worship event. I would consistently receive feedback from adults telling me that they could see the Spirit in me (I didn't know what that meant, but I liked hearing it!), that I had a mind of my own in worship. If the whole choir was making a coordinated effort to sway to the left, I would have none of it if the

Spirit was leading me to the right! There are things I was able to understand about God in the context of music that I would not have been able to capture by just thinking or talking about God. People have told me that while I was in college, they could hear the echoes of Gospel music through the walls of my dorm room. The people who lived with me knew that living with me included becoming acquainted with the music I had loved growing up, the music that had taught me so much about God.

While attending the University of Dallas, as my respect and love for the Catholic Faith grew, it was also through music that I was able again to encounter God in an incredibly meaningful way. This time, it was singing Latin liturgical music with the Collegium Cantorum through the university. That music, much like Gospel music, remains dear to me today and is a reason it breaks my heart to see folks on either side of the ridiculous Catholic aisle we have set up (liberal and conservative) weaponize Latin, as either a sign of superior right-minded holiness and worship or a sign of apostasy and fanaticism. For me, it was something that required me to sit down and look more closely at what this music was saying to me, because I did not know Latin, and so had to take time to translate what I was singing. It was the vehicle or means God used to break open for me the traditions of the Church, the liturgical seasons, the glory of the Mass itself. It was a gift that I would have failed to honor if I had used it to inflate my religious ego, prop myself up as superior to other Catholics, and cover my insecurities in pursuing holiness. It was a gift, not some sign of fanaticism or apostasy from the pope or the Second Vatican Council. It was simply a gift from the Church.

Singing that music with my friends catapulted me into a deeper understanding of God. As we worshiped together, inviting others to worship and giving praise to God, I grew in a deep understanding and appreciation for the liturgical seasons, especially of Lent, Holy Week, and Easter. Once again, through music I was able to learn about God. I recently had an opportunity to briefly reunite with a couple of members from that choir and step into a beautiful church, much like the ones we sang in as we traveled through Europe. As we walked together through the church, a liturgical choir began to practice in the choir loft, and our eyes instantly filled with tears. The music was then and is now a sign of the gift of faith that it ushered in for us, and our tears were of pure gratitude for this gift and for one another — to have each other's eyes to look into and confirm that the mystery of this gift is indeed real.

So, Saint Cecilia, I have to say, was my first "saint love," and the clear and obvious choice for my confirmation patron because of the central role of music in my faith journey. She taught me that the saints we love and befriend, in many cases, choose us long before we choose them. They join God in His pursuit of us. I believe Saint Cecilia was praying for me and working on me long before I knew her. Once we discover our friends, we then enter into their stories, and it is in their stories, much more than in only their patronage, that we encounter their witness of hope. I chose her as my patron with very shallow knowledge of her story. She was a woman sitting at an organ representing her patronage of music. But there's another image of her that evokes a greater sense of Christian hope. The more authentic image would be seeing her placed in a bath by the prefect of Rome, Turcius Almachius, a bath that is hot with flames, in the hopes that she would be burned alive as a punishment for preaching the Faith, only to survive those flames, and then also survive, for

THE SAINTS WE LOVE AND BEFRIEND, IN MANY CASES, CHOOSE US LONG BEFORE WE CHOOSE THEM. THEY JOIN GOD IN HIS PURSUIT OF US.

three days, with three blows to her neck that were an attempt to behead her. And in those three days, as she bled and suffered, she continued to preach and pray as she had throughout her life, continuing to convert men and women to Christianity, adding to the almost 400 people she had already helped God convert to the Faith. What an incredible image of hope!

The entire life of a saint becomes an act of hope, and this is why the Church presents these men and women to us as models of Christian living — and dying.

The next saints to choose me were St. Josephine Bakhita and Saint Joseph, stepfather of Jesus. As soon as I realized that God might be calling me to religious life, and I learned that would give me an opportunity to change my name, I was thrilled. I always disliked my baptismal name, Toni. Just Toni. It wasn't short for anything. It was just Toni. I wanted something more extravagant, I wanted something more feminine, and so this chance to change my name was like a religious life party favor! I toyed with the most extravagant and feminine names I could think of that I could tell some sort of prayerful story in connection with so it didn't look like this was entirely an effort of vanity (which it was). I landed for a good amount of time on the name Veronica Simon, and was again thrilled at the hope of one day being called something as lovely as Veronica. As the time for entrance into the novitiate and the taking of a new name approached, here came the saints again, breaking into my reality, or rather bringing reality into my fantasy.

I was sitting in our convent chapel, spending time in adoration before morning prayer like I had done hundreds of mornings before. It was Advent, and I was praying with a reflection that focused on Saint Joseph. I will never forget how a piece of Saint Joseph's life and identity pierced my heart in prayer that morning. In almost an instant, the depth of his humanity struck me with a fullness it never had before. I became aware that while he seemed in the shadows of the Holy Family, in a way, he was also the star of the Holy Family, precisely because of his simplicity, his quietness, and his obedience. He was not immaculately conceived, he was not God, and yet, he held space for the Immaculate Conception and God-made-man to flourish among us. He was the first to allow this great mystery of the Church's relationship with God in Mary to abide in the world. Something about this simple realization that morning brought about in my heart an affection for Saint Joseph that I have never been able to shake since then; and just as simply as the idea to be a religious sister had floated into my mind years before, in that moment, in the same way, the name Josephine floated into my mind. Nope! I recognized that voice of God in prayer, and I immediately knew what was happening. I abruptly stopped and thought, *Nope, it is Veronica. Veronica Simon to be exact.* Yet, just like before, each way I turned, all I could think was *Josephine.* I had also had a sincere, lasting, and earnest desire to have a name connected to our Mother Foundress of the Sisters of the Holy Family of Nazareth, Frances Siedliska; but I knew there was nothing Frances-y about me, so I did not venture down that road. When it was time to submit a name request to my superiors, I could only write to request the name Josephine, because each day since that morning of prayer, it had impressed itself upon my heart more and more.

Then the question arose: What day would be my feast day? I had two options with Saint Joseph, as well as the option to have a feast day for St. Josephine Bakhita. Well, who was this Josephine Bakhita? A beautiful Black woman, born in Sudan and enslaved throughout her youth, the survivor of evil and crimes against her humanity, including sexual assault. Upon arrival in Italy with a family who claimed to own her, she began to learn about God, whom she would rightly name as her only Master. When the family who claimed to own her sought to take her from Italy, she asserted her freedom and desire to remain with the sisters who had been teaching her about God; and that is what she did. She would later become a religious sister, and she died after many years of service as a sister. Her life and the scars on her body told of the suffering she had endured, and yet one of the quotes she is most famous for is, "The whole of my life has been God's gift." I eventually chose the feast day of March 19

SAINT JOSEPH IS THE FIRST WITNESS TO HOPE.

(Saint Joseph's feast day), since my original inspiration for the name was the gift of prayer of Saint Joseph. But love for Saint Josephine has only grown in me, and she is the patron of my office where I practice as a counselor. Her image and that famous quote hang on the wall.

Saint Joseph is the first witness to hope. Our hope is born in the Resurrection, and without the relationship that the Spirit has with the Blessed Virgin Mary, our resurrection would not be a possibility. Saint Joseph was the first to bear witness to this hope, to testify to it with his obedience and faith when he took Mary as his wife. He witnessed hope growing in her womb, and he witnessed hope born in the fullness of time. He witnessed hope grow in "wisdom and age and favor before God and man" (Lk 2:52). St. Josephine Bakhita was a witness to hope because she was able to allow the Gospel and her relationship with Jesus to transform her suffering from definitive to redemptive. She recognized that God did not create her, become man, live in this world, die on a cross, lie in a tomb, rise from the dead, tabernacle in this world risen for forty days, ascend to the Father, send His Spirit, and continue to dwell among us in the Eucharist so she could be defined by the abuses and sins against her humanity that she suffered. He did all that so that she would be defined by Him, and hope in Him, through Him, and with Him. When she proclaims that the *whole* of her life has been a gift, she does not do this as some Pollyanna we can roll our eyes and shrug our shoulders at; she proclaims it as a woman standing in full stature in the Faith, knowing that with Christ, even scars give glory.

And what of the desire to have a name connected to my mother foundress, Bl. Mary of Jesus the Good Shepherd, born Frances Siedliska, a Polish noblewoman who would found and lead an international congregation centered on the love of the Holy Family and spreading that love in the world? After I turned in my request for the name Josephine, seemingly letting go not only of "Veronica Simon" but also the lingering desire to have a name connected to Mother Foundress, I was reviewing facts about her life for a class, working to commit them to memory, and I came across her full baptismal name, which I had forgotten: Frances Anna Josephine. We are in the care of the saints, not the other way around.

THE SAINTS RUN ALONGSIDE GOD IN PURSUIT OF OUR SOULS.

I could really do this all day. I could recount more and more canonized saints or beatified blesseds who have chosen me, who have cared for me, who have reached for me and helped me to see what hope is really about through their stories of fidelity and heroic virtue, who have helped me to see what God's hopes are for me, what He hopes to accomplish in this life that He has given to me and that He sustains in His will. The saints run alongside God in pursuit of our souls. They reveal, like Saint Cecilia did for me all those years ago, a concern that God has for the details of our lives. Bl. Carlo Acutis is the patron of youth computer programmers! God cares about computer programming and gaming! He wants even that to be sanctified for His glory.

At the end of the day, these people, as Pope Francis says, are not perfect models, but persons, whom I would call friends, run through by God. They don't point us to themselves with their stories, but they always point to God. They are like stained glass, allowing the one light to flow through their many shades. The many shades are absolutely key. The saints prove to us that we belong in this Church. That the sacraments are for all. You don't have to have one specific sort of story to be at home in the Church, you just have to say yes to His story, and live that yes through a participation in the sacramental life of the Church. The baptismal font is open for you. The confessional door is open for you. The Eucharistic table is for all who desire it enough to prepare themselves for it. I was visiting with a friend once who was frustrated with how hard and time-consuming it can be for people to be prepared to receive the Eucharist, to which I responded that we see people spend a full year preparing to walk in a cotillion, or the East Texas Rose Festival, or run in a marathon. Why is about nine months of preparation to receive Jesus in the Eucharist — Body, Blood, Soul and Divinity — a stretch? The Church is yours; brown, black, yellow, whatever shade you may be, it is yours, and the saints prove that to us as they show forth their many shades illuminated with the light of God. But these friends of ours are not only in heaven. Can we be bold enough and have enough kingdom vision to recognize the saints in our own lives?

For me, that vision has included my aunt and uncle. My aunt is no perfect model, as she will quickly have choice words for someone who decides to cross her, and she has a fuse the size of my pinky fingernail; yet, she will also serve the poor around her without hesitation. And I am not talking about that distant service of the poor we sometimes do, where we keep them nameless and at a distance, I mean *in her home*. She has made room in our home for more struggling people than I have been able to count. My uncle has joined together with her in that mission to serve the poor as well. He is also no perfect model, but he will be the one to stop on the road when he sees someone stranded and help them. He will be the adult to get on the floor and play with kids when all the other adults in the room can't really be bothered. Together, they are saints.

My best friend's mother, when she was physically fading because of cancer, took that time as an opportunity to serve others and proclaim the presence of Jesus in the midst of ordinary experiences. She shared stories with me about seeing people who were sick willing to help others, and it made her also want to help others in the midst of her own suffering, and she would end each story in her lovely Paraguayan accent, saying to me, "That's the Jesus, Toni." She demanded a Catholic funeral Mass in her final requests, a demand that was odd for her to make to her daughters who were not practicing Catholics, but one she didn't hesitate to make, and I was able to understand why, because daughters aside, "that's the Jesus." She had returned to the Mass and celebration of the sacraments after building a relationship with a South American priest at her local parish. She is a saint.

A mentor I met when I was a candidate with the sisters and fundraising through the Labouré Society ministry for vocations blocked by student loan debt, who was physically full of life, clearly mindful regarding his health, and dead serious about his faith, would later go on to lose his physical abilities, becoming quadriplegic due to shocking and unexpected health difficulties. He would go on to describe this time as a time of deepening his faith, and would not fail to lose the lift of joy and hope in his voice despite massive suffering. He is a saint. He would hate to hear me describe him that way, and even so, he is a saint.

I think of my sister Margaret, who died when I was a candidate with the sisters — who, I would learn, in her final days in the bed in her room, asked one of our sisters to visit her, and asked that sister to please take care of me and ensure I always felt welcome in Nazareth. A woman on her deathbed worried about me, basically a stranger to her, who had lived with her for only a matter of months, included me, my well-being, and concern for my vocation in her last wishes, while she could have instead been preoccupied with her pain. She is a saint.

These are all saints who have walked and do walk in the flesh in my life, like all the saints have walked in this world: in the flesh. When I call them saints, I am not disregarding the wisdom of the Church in her processes for beatification and canonization. I am not implying our subjective opinions can hijack the wise processes of the Church. I am instead turning toward the ability of these people to witness to hope with their very lives. To, in all circumstances, look to the hills from whence comes their help (see Ps 121:1). In suffering and sickness, when the poor are stretched far outside of comfort, when it seems like they have left behind a life of participation in the sacraments, only to turn and cling to them with the last days of their life — this is the stuff of hope. And we have people walking in our midst who can reveal it to us when it seems far off. God is active in them, God is active in the saints, a light breaking through into the darkness.

GOD IS ACTIVE IN THE SAINTS, A LIGHT BREAKING THROUGH INTO THE DARKNESS.

One of my newest saint friends, a recent love, is Servant of God Julia Greeley, Denver's Angel of Charity, a Black Catholic woman who lived out her life in Denver, Colorado, after being freed from enslavement in Missouri. She served the poor, worshiped regularly via participation in the sacraments, and had a beautiful devotion to the Sacred Heart of Jesus and the Eucharist. She was known for ministering to firefighters in Denver, and also for providing for the poor from her own poverty. She was described as a one-woman St. Vincent de Paul ministry. Once I came to know her, I resolved that I would visit her remains in the Denver cathedral at the first opportunity I got. One of my sisters and I made a day of it, a sort of Servant of God Julia Greeley pilgrimage day. The conclusion of the pilgrimage was to pray at her burial place in the Denver cathedral, but before that, we visited the parish in town where she worshiped, sat in what was believed to be her pew, walked to the physical address that was where her home would have been, and fittingly found in the exact spot of that address a mural of Breonna Taylor, a young Black woman who was wrongly killed by police officers, surrounded with roses. Then we made our way to the cathedral.

I walked in by myself (Sister had let me out while she parked the car and made a phone call). I was walking around the cathedral, uncertain where Julia's tomb might be, when a Black man approached me with a whimsical, joyful look on his face. He exclaimed, "Are you a nun? I have never seen a Black nun!" To which I responded, "Well, here I am!" with a joyful smile also on my face. He asked me questions about myself and my vocation, and I answered them and then shared with him why I was there and invited him to find Julia with me. We began to walk together, and he asked me why he so rarely saw images in Catholic churches that were not white. I told him that I did not have an answer, but that I was sorry that it was that way, because God surely did not intend the Catholic Church to appear to be only one race. He said that was his main problem with the Catholic Church, that he could not see himself in it or find anyone there who looked like him, or looked like they could have led a life like his. Then we found the remains of Servant of God Julia Greeley, at the very front of the cathedral. I told him who she was and that I had come there to ask her to pray for me and my intentions. By then, my sister had joined me and also met him. Together, we explained the reasoning and purpose behind intercessory prayer and told him he was welcome to pray with us. He said, "No ... I don't think so ... well ... wait ... that is *really* a Black woman in there?" I told him, "Yes." And he said, "You know there are some things I want to ask her help with."

The first thing I did at the tomb of Servant of God Julia Greeley was watch a Black man who had never prayed intercessory prayers in his life, had been uncertain about the Church herself because he couldn't see himself in it, kneel before her remains and ask for her prayers for healing for his cancer and help through his treatments. Sister and I audibly wept, and then also knelt to pray our own prayers. Servant of God Julia Greeley, such an important shade of color in the stained glass of the saints, each bearing the light in her own shades.

I want to be a saint. I don't know what kind I will be. I know it is going to be in the misfit, wayward category, and that will be just fine, as long as I am a saint. I know it is happening and will only happen in the relationship crucible. Relationships are what make saints. Sometimes I joke with people and tell them my goal is purgatory. But that is a lie. However, it is less painful

RELATIONSHIPS ARE WHAT MAKE SAINTS.

and is safer than admitting that I want to be a saint, because once they know that I really want to be a saint, they are way more in tune with the ways I am just not there yet at all. But I do want to be a saint. Say that right now sincerely to yourself: Say, "I want to be a saint," and see if the slight sting that comes along with admitting that desire pierces your heart. That's hope — that piercing longing that mingles with delight and joy. Sometimes being a saint seems far off, and then there are some brief moments where it seems possible.

We are often so quick to highlight the moments in our lives where we have been far off the mark of sainthood, but I would like to challenge you to highlight for yourself those moments when you let the light shine through, when you let yourself be run through by God and manifest in the world the reality that the kingdom is here even as it is coming; that it is being born. Hold fast and highlight in your mind the moments when you let the light pass through all the shades and colors of you, of your story — the obvious areas, the hidden areas. Reflect on those moments; take hold of them. This isn't arrogance or a lack of humility. This isn't navel-gazing. It is a turn toward God and an act of thanksgiving for His faithful work in you. Take hold of the moments where you received God's light in your heart and transmitted it to the world. Once you've done that, then do it more. Let's all do it more. Let's hope like saints. Let's hope to be saints. Let's witness to hope — or Hope, rather, because our Hope is a Person, born of a woman.

6

OUR LADY: SHE WHO LABORS IN HOPE

I am in labor again with all the children of God, until Jesus Christ my Son be formed in them in the fullness of His age.

— *St. Louis de Montfort,* True Devotion to Mary

I am glad I am not the vehicle for my own salvation — the train, the carriage, whatever transport I will use on the bumpy ride to heaven. I would be in trouble. Looking back, I know now that I was raised by a woman who was devoted to the Blessed Virgin Mary, but when I was little, I was clueless about this. My aunt had been raised Catholic in a small country in the Caribbean, Dominica. I have had the privilege of visiting this beautiful Catholic country twice, and I hope one day to be able to return now that I am Catholic myself, so that I can attend Mass at the church in the town, Massacre (pronounced mah-sack), where she is from. The church is at the top of a monstrous hill, which is probably right and just! I can look back now and see that my aunt had surrounded herself with rosaries, and she prayed with them often, even though once she had arrived in the United States, she was no longer attending a Catholic church. We all went together as a family to our Baptist church; however, I know well now how much she continued to foster a Catholic life of prayer — praying the Rosary and praying novenas and doing her morning prayer devotionals. But again, as a kid, I had no idea.

People often ask me how I developed my relationship with the Blessed Virgin Mary as a convert. They will ask how I handled the big change of now having the opportunity to have a devotion to her, which is not common in the Protestant experience. To be honest, at first, I just sort of ignored her! I was well aware that the Blessed Virgin Mary was central in our Faith, but I just didn't entertain the idea very much. The first time I spent any real time reflecting on Mary was when I was visiting La Madeleine Catholic Church in France. I was not Catholic yet. I was traveling with my college choir, and we had some free time to spend in the church, so I sat down for some quiet time and found myself in front of a statue of the Blessed Virgin Mary. The statue was colorless, all white marble. For some reason, I stared at this image of the Blessed Virgin Mary longer than was usual for me, and it dawned on me that the woman in the statue appeared to be pregnant. Something about that made this image of Mary very attractive to me, in a way others had not yet been. After that, our relationship would return to dormancy for quite some time.

As I was growing in formation, learning to be a religious sister and learning the rule for our congregation, the Sisters of the Holy Family of Nazareth, I became aware of our love for Mary as a congregation. In our statutes we are asked to pray the Rosary daily. In the words of our Mother Foundress and in our constitutions, we are asked to foster a sincere relationship with Mary, and all our names are actually Mary! Each sister is required to have some reference to the Blessed Virgin in her name. This is usually done by formally having the name Mary in front of the chosen name (for example, my formal name is Mary Josephine), or by including a reference to Mary in another way, like Sr. Pia Marie or Sr. Maria Thérèse.

There are months throughout the year during which we add additional Marian devotions to our common prayers. I was no longer able to simply ignore the presence of this woman in my faith.

I WAS NO LONGER ABLE TO SIMPLY IGNORE THE PRESENCE OF THIS WOMAN IN MY FAITH.

Looking back, I can see that I was bothered by how she was presented to me in art throughout time. I found myself, a Black, animated, heavy-set woman, constantly standing before images of a stick-thin woman with pale, white skin, sometimes light eyes and light hair, with next to no expression on her face. And she was supposed to be my mother? I was supposed to be her daughter? I found myself standing before manger scenes that could not possibly ever have experienced the stench of a living animal, let alone the stench of the messiness of real life, and I could not put myself in there, I could not possibly belong there. It was like if I entered into her life or allowed her to enter into mine, I would somehow make a mess of what the world presented to me as pristine. I have increasing frustration with how we have managed to sanitize our Faith and the concept of holiness through art. What is holy is so often depicted as lifeless, emotionless, and sterile. And while what has been created fits the norms of beauty we have become entrenched in, it slowly edges us and our own realities out of the realm of holiness depicted for us in art. What would have been the reality of the cave at the birth of Jesus? Not silence, but the joyful wails of a living, thriving, healthy newborn child. The tears as Mary gave birth to this child. The bewilderment, joy, and amazement that would have been on the face of Joseph. Perhaps there was joyful laughter through tears. Conversations with shepherds and kings. The elements, the weather, the wind, the heat, so present, because they could not shelter in an inn. The animals, their stench, bugs. Right there in the midst of this utter realness, Love took on flesh, God dwelt. Nothing of what I had seen of Marian art taught me about the gritty holiness of this woman who could bear forth immaculate life in the meanest and most crude of circumstances.

The novitiate for me was the time in my life when my Mother stood right before me and made me understand who she is. It began with a reflection I was assigned to listen to on the Gospel according to Matthew. I had often heard that Matthew chose to reference women in his genealogy as a sign of the feminism to come. That never resonated with me, but seemed like a needy imposition of modern thought on Scripture — a shallow, self-centered, stubborn reading of Scripture desperate to make sense of a man-made approach to understanding ourselves, rather than seeking to be docile recipients of understanding ourselves according to what God has to say about us, allowing God to impose upon us His truths. As I began listening to the study (it was on CDs!), the presenter provided context to Matthew's genealogy. He explained that the Jewish people, to whom Matthew was ministering, would have struggled with suspicion surrounding Mary's pregnancy. He went on to explain, instead of trying to prove to his listeners Mary's perfection, Matthew instead inclined them to the history they already believed: that the bloodline of salvation had been pulled through imperfect women in the past, so if they in fact believed Mary to be imperfect, why would that imperfection stop the line of salvation now? The presenter noted that Matthew's ongoing use of the words "fourteen generations" implied an ongoing reference back to the promise of David, because the same word for *fourteen* at the time was also the word *David*. So, it was as though Matthew was repeating to them over and over again, "David, David, David, through Mary comes the descendant of David." This intrigued me, and the glimmer of attraction to the Blessed Virgin I had felt sitting before that French statue of her appearing to be pregnant was reignited.

As I entered into the second quarter of my second year in the novitiate, it was time to begin work on my application for first vows. It is customary to write a letter of request for vows, and as I began to draft that letter, it dawned on me that learning about Mary had somehow provided me with a framework to understand what was at work in me in my own vocation. I was shocked by this letter pouring forth my gratitude for the example of her life and her Magnificat song. As I wrote, I realized that the Magnificat had become for me a way to not only understand what was at work in me as a growing religious sister, but to feel confident about it, and to wrap my mind and hands around it. A few months later, the deal was sealed.

Throughout the novitiate, I would spend regular time at Marytown in Libertyville, Illinois. I would go there and pray before the relics of St. Maximillian Kolbe, spend time in adoration before the five-foot monstrance that perpetually holds the Blessed Sacrament in the main church, and learn more and more about Mary. One day, in the gift shop, I saw a box full of one-dollar books. I dug down in the box, thrilled because I love collecting spiritual books. I found there a book that was a guide to consecration to Jesus through Mary that would take thirty-three days. I had heard of other people making a consecration to Mary, and the thought had been on my mind (way, way in the back of my mind). The book was only a dollar, so I thought, *Why not?* Today, it breaks my heart to know that growing that relationship was worth only a dollar to me; today, I would give really anything to know her more intimately. I told myself that I would complete the consecration before the day of my first vows, if I remembered to get started in time. Then I placed my one-dollar book on the shelf and forgot about it. One day, while sitting in my chair in my room, I wondered about the consecration book, but I was certain I had let too much time go by and that my vows were less than the needed thirty-four days away. I pulled the book off the shelf and began to count. If I began that day, on the exact date of my first vows, I would also complete the consecration to Jesus through Mary. So, I began.

In the pages of that book, I learned about an aspect of Mary's identity I had never known. I knew she is a mother to Jesus, a daughter to God the Father, but now I learned that to the Spirit, she is a spouse. I believed deeply in the Spirit, and the spark that had been in me before that statue in France was aflame. I realized that what the Spirit wants to occur in the flesh is born in the womb of Mary. I would later read it far more eloquently in St. Louis de Montfort's *Total Consecration to Jesus through Mary*:

"I am in labor again with all the children of God, until Jesus Christ my Son be formed in them in the fullness of His age." Saint Augustine, surpassing himself and going beyond all I have yet said, affirms that all the predestinate, in order to be conformed to the image of the Son of God, are in this world hidden in the womb of the most holy Virgin, where they are guarded, nourished, brought up and made to grow by that good Mother until she has brought them forth to glory after death, which is properly the day of their birth.

I was completely captivated and inspired. Mary is far from some delicate, lifeless, bland statue on a mantel. She is fierce, aflame with the fire of the Spirit, the Mother of all life, courageous in constant labor, so near to the pains, sufferings, joys, and victories in the world that it in a sense is all happening right in her flesh. She puts flesh on the work of her spouse, the Holy

SHE PUTS FLESH ON THE WORK OF HER SPOUSE, THE HOLY SPIRIT, AS SHE LABORS STILL TODAY.

Spirit, as she labors still today. She is wild, in the very best way. A wild availability and motherhood, born in obedience, faith, and trust, that sets her free and unleashes the gifts of her Immaculate Heart, making her wildly and radically mother of all. She is strong and patient with us, her children, who are ignorant and slow to learn of her love as she carries us to heaven. She is a model for me to follow as a religious sister, a model for understanding the fruit of celibacy and of the vows. I find a home in her (literally!). I am no longer alienated from my Mother, but can see that she is not so perfect that she is far off from me. No, she is perfect in the sense that she is like me enough that she can help me to be like her, and that she is near. Just like a child is ignorant that he grows in his mother's womb and is not himself the impetus for their relationship, so it is with us; our relationship with Mary is not our doing, it is already her doing. We simply receive, and over time, we learn to love our Mother.

I shared before that I struggled to hope for a good portion of my life. I am grateful that with the help of therapy and spiritual direction, I was able to pinpoint some significant moments in my life when I gave up on hope or lost hope. Most of them are from when I was a young girl, and honestly, I was tempted to recount them for you here, but I cannot, out of love and reverence for my loved ones. What I will say is this: In those moments, when I unlearned hope, I thought that hope was lost. I later learned this was not possible. I was on a thirty-day silent retreat, preparing now for final vows. My relationship with Mary had flourished so much that I was aware now that she would be the subject of my final vows mystery, but why and under what title was still a mystery to me! A "final vows mystery" is a phrase that a religious sister adds to the end of her name when she makes final vows. It is a descriptive phrase of how God has come to her over time, perhaps throughout her life, or throughout her discernment in religious life. So, for example, Thérèse of the Child Jesus has as her mystery the Child Jesus. We have a Sr. Marietta of Jesus Christ Crucified, a Sr. Mary Emmanuela of God Who is Faithful, a Sr. Mary Faustina of the Eternal Love of the Sacred Heart of Jesus, and so on. A huge part of my thirty-day retreat was reflecting on how my own final vows mystery was to take shape. I was in the days of the retreat where I was praying through the death of Jesus, and I was in the company of Mary during those days. We were together in prayer at the foot of the cross, and the love of Jesus in that moment impressed upon me in a profound way.

I felt sorrow for all the love of Jesus that I had wasted, and that we all waste — how much love goes unnoticed, how perfectly divine He was in the moment He gave His life, the most powerful expression of His divinity, and how often I wasted that. In prayer, I perceived a correction from Mary: Mary would not allow her Son's love to be wasted, to return to Him void (see Is 55:11). She instead holds it in her womb until we are ready to receive it and for it to be born in our lives, to bear fruit in our lives. In prayer, Mary and I eventually buried Jesus in the tomb, and then in prayer it was as if she and I were in the garden where Jesus' tomb was. I imagined Mary walking around in that garden, praying, waiting, and hoping. Memories of being a young girl who had given up on hope floated into my mind. Toward the end of the retreat, I was asked to pray the meditation written by Saint

Ignatius called "Contemplation to Attain the Love of God." I will describe this meditation in more detail later. For now, I will just say briefly that in this meditation, the retreatant is asked to look at the world in light of the Resurrection and join with Jesus in His mission. When I met Jesus there, I was a little girl, a little girl who was full of hope, the little girl who had been willing to hope in situations where it seemed silly to do so. Again, the vision of myself as a little girl who had given up on hope floated into my mind. Then it dawned on me that hope is never lost. It doesn't disappear or die when our hearts are broken or when we become too afraid to hope. Mary, the Mother of all hope, because of her relationship to the Spirit, holds it for us, and she had held it for me, laboring, and it had drawn me to her.

HOPE IS NEVER LOST. IT DOESN'T DISAPPEAR OR DIE WHEN OUR HEARTS ARE BROKEN OR WHEN WE BECOME TOO AFRAID TO HOPE.

All that we hope for is abiding right beneath her Immaculate Heart, waiting to be born into the world through each one of us — ultimately the new heaven and the new earth, where she will reign as Queen.

Again, I ask you: Are there areas of your life where you are afraid to hope? How can Mary be helpful to you there? I have always believed that the mysteries of the Rosary are actually the story of her life, but she is so Christ-centered that it looks mostly like the story of Christ's life. Still, if we look carefully, chronologically, the mysteries of the Rosary begin and end with her experiences: from the Annunciation to her Coronation. If you had to come up with your own Rosary mysteries of your life, that were centered on Christ, what would be your sorrowful, joyful, luminous, and glorious mysteries? If you had to pick a mystery for your life like a religious sister's final vows mystery, a way that

God has come to you continually over the years, what would it be? I invite you to place yourself before an image of the Blessed Virgin Mary that resonates with you and ask your Mother to help you answer any or all of these questions. She will not leave you unaided — be inspired by this confidence.

My final vows mystery is the Espoused Mother of our Eucharistic King. Indeed, she is the spouse of the Spirit, and indeed her Son reigns as King in the Eucharist.

7

THE EUCHARIST: THE SLOW WORK OF GOD

Above all, trust in the slow work of God.

— *Pierre Teilhard de Chardin, SJ*

Pope Benedict XVI once wrote, "God loves us; we need only to summon up the humility to let ourselves be loved." He wrote this following a beautiful comparison of the Holy Thursday washing of the feet to the work of the Eucharist in our lives. Have you ever had your feet washed on Holy Thursday, as a part of remembering what Jesus did for the disciples on the night of the Last Supper? I highly recommend that families and groups of believers begin and maintain the tradition of washing one another's feet on or close to Holy Thursday. Sit down together with a Bible, a basin of water, and some towels (and some replacement water for when the basin fills with dirty water!). Read the Gospel of Saint John chapter 13, verses 1 through 20, and then simply and quietly (as quietly as is realistic for your family) wash one another's feet, and ensure you allow your feet to be washed.

The first time I had my feet washed in a setting like this, in a liturgical manner if you will, I would like to say my response had a lot to do with the lack of preparation I had for what I had gotten myself into. But in reality, it was honestly more about what Cardinal Joseph Ratzinger mentioned, a struggle to let myself be loved. The invitation to have my feet washed by a friend who was being Jesus to me stripped away the veneer I had put in place to hide the difficulty I had with receiving love. I had gathered at the home of the parents of my dear friends. Their parents would later go on to be parents to me, as I would call them godparents. It was Holy Thursday, and I was told we would be washing one another's feet in remembrance of what Jesus did for the disciples and commanded us to do for one another. My godfather read the Gospel of John for all of us, and then we were told the order in which the washing would progress. As I watched members of the family kneel before other members and quietly wash their feet, followed by an almost whispered "Thank you" in each case, tears began to fall from my eyes. And then, my friend from college knelt before me, took my feet, placed them in a bowl with a towel across his lap, and did his best to imitate Jesus. I was completely undone. I did not know where to hold this kind of charity. All I could do was sob. It has taken years for me to understand those tears, and I do not think I am done understanding them, but I believe that moment planted a seed of faith in me that had a Eucharistic character.

I would go on to have countless more encounters with Jesus

in the Eucharist. The first time I received the Eucharist, I cried so hard someone asked me if I had caught the Holy Ghost. To which I answered, well, actually yes, because I had received the Sacrament of Confirmation that evening! After becoming Catholic, I was thrilled by opportunities to receive the Eucharist. I was transitioning between jobs when I became Catholic, and I took the opportunity during those days of not working to attend daily Mass as often as I could; I just wanted to receive Jesus. I was growing in love for the Eucharist through all these encounters and opportunities to receive Holy Communion, but there was something about this one day in February 2009, something different about my encounter with Jesus in the Eucharist that day, that made it feel like a first encounter. I was sitting in a gym serving as a chaperone for a youth retreat. I had been Catholic about four years now and had just a few months earlier returned from a trip to Rome with members of the Latin liturgical choir I sang with while I was in college. That trip provided an opportunity for the work that God had begun in me when I received the sacraments to be deepened significantly. I had the opportunity to return to Saint Peter's Basilica, which I had first visited as a University of Dallas sophomore living in Rome for a semester.

WHEN I FINISHED, THE PRIEST OFFERED ME ONLY TWO WORDS: "JUST BEGIN."

During that choir trip, some friends and I had decided to sort of recreate our experience of seeing Saint Peter's for the first time as college students by arriving at the basilica right when the doors opened, because at that time the sun was rising, and it felt like you had the whole place to yourself. What was different this time was that I walked through those doors as a confirmed Catholic. I was able to go to confession and Mass there in Saint Peter's that morning.

When I knelt down to make my confession, I became overwhelmed with gratitude, and the confession that flowed from my heart was much more about the things I knew God was calling me to do and I was disobediently refusing to do, instead of being about the things I had done. I confessed all the ways I had felt convicted to work to grow in my faith and in service to the Church, and all the ways I had ignored those promptings of the Spirit. It was like a litany, and when I finished, the priest offered me only two words: "Just begin." Then he asked me to make my act of contrition. So, just begin is what I did, in multiple ways, one of them being by returning from Rome and signing up to be a small group leader and chaperone with my college roommate's parish youth group, where she served as a youth minister. There I was that day, just beginning, and feeling incredibly grateful that God had purified my desires, and that there, chaperoning youth, was where I wanted to be. It wasn't based on duty; my desires aligned with God's desires, and it was a wonderful experience.

The youth participating in the retreat spent most of the day gathered around a structure that had the exposed Blessed Sacrament on the top. When they took a break, I took that opportunity to say some prayers of my own before the Blessed Sacrament. In spiritual direction, I was learning to pray and also learning to pray about what God might be calling me to vocationally. That day I was not preoccupied with telling God what I thought my vocation was and then praying that He make it happen for me (which is often what our vocational prayers shape up to be. *God, go get me everything I decided that I deserve because I shouldn't have to settle for "less"* — meanwhile we miss that it is not about less or more, but about receiving from God what He has in mind for us). That day, I didn't have time for that; my heart was entirely too preoccupied with gratitude. I sat before the Blessed Sacrament, Jesus in the Eucharist, and let prayers of thanksgiving flow freely from my heart. *Thank you, Jesus, for allowing me to be in this place with these young people. Thank you, Jesus, for the grace to be joyful about being here and for purifying my desires to prefer this over a Netflix binge, because I am certain God did not make man for the Netflix binge! Thank you, Jesus, for being here in the Eucharist. Thank you, Jesus, for the gift of faith.* And then — *It would be so cool to be a sister and serve the Church this way!* My eyes flew open, and I wondered why I would ever think such a thing. And just to make sure it was impressed upon my senses, at that exact moment a religious sister walked by, her veil and habit flowing just enough for me to feel a very slight breeze. There was the Church again, filling up my senses.

I did what anyone would do when they become more fully aware of an interest in religious life; I jumped up and walked out of the presence of Jesus in the Eucharist. I was certain He had misunderstood my prayers! I walked outside to just get a grip because at this point, I knew enough about God to know that that was certainly not nothing. My plan was to take a minute alone in the parking lot, thinking that was where I would be least likely to run into anyone, and of course, there was my college roommate walking right toward me. She could see from my facial expression that I was upset, and she asked me what was up. I told her the truth, and then she, with a directness I will never forget, asked me if I felt called to religious life. I lied. And then I told the truth; I told her I really didn't know.

I spent the rest of the day disturbed. Let me pause here and say this: Culturally, in our Church, we are beginning to relegate encounters with Jesus in the Eucharist to those which are emotionally pleasant or consoling. But the Eucharistic presence is also a disturbance, and rightly so! It is the Incarnation not just breaking forth into time, but breaking forth into each one of us, conforming us to the likeness of Christ and bringing us into one in Jesus. This is a remodel. This is a restoration. If you have ever remodeled your home, you know it can be quite the disturbing mess before things are lovely. While absolutely, sometimes our encounter with Jesus in the Eucharist will be emotionally pleasant and consoling, it will also be a disturbance to our plans and our realities, and this is right and just and about so much more than our emotions. That day, *disturbed* was the only word for my experience. Unsettled, shaken up, thinking why on earth would I have thought something like that, where did it come from, and why did it shake me up so much! I still considered myself a very new Catholic. Up until that point, I was a Sunday Mass-goer and then did what I wanted in between Sundays.

THE EUCHARISTIC PRESENCE IS ALSO A DISTURBANCE, AND RIGHTLY SO!

I had spent next to no time growing in knowledge of my Faith once RCIA had ended four years earlier. If one of the youth had asked me to name the gold thing holding the Blessed Sacrament, I would not have been able to tell them that it was a monstrance. How could someone who did know the word monstrance be thinking about being a religious sister? How could someone who was trying to do a little "just beginning" all of a sudden be haunted by a whole lot more than "just beginning"?

The sun had set, the youth had heard more talks, and then we were being prepared for something I had never seen and did not understand. The priests told us that they were going to walk around the room with the gold thing holding Jesus, and that there would be a garment falling from it toward the ground. They told us that Jesus walked among us today in the Eucharist just as powerfully as when He walked among us during his thirty-three years on earth, including the few years of his public ministry. They told us He could heal each of us tonight as He healed then, and that we were free to reach out and touch His garment as the hemorrhaging woman in the Gospel did and pray for healing that we needed. The lights were dimmed, and the only significant light was a spotlight on Jesus in the Eucharist. I could not take my eyes off Jesus. I tried, because I felt odd, but the need to keep my eyes fixed on Jesus superseded discomfort about feeling odd. Everywhere Jesus went, I watched and watched. And then I saw people worshiping in all sorts of various ways. It was how I had grown up. In our Baptist church people worshiped as they saw fit, some standing, some sitting, some arms outstretched, some kneeling.

I looked to my right and saw a middle-aged white man in professional clothes prostrate on the ground waiting for Jesus, and at the sight of it I became undone. I wish today that I could thank that man; his reverence was the key that allowed the last scale to drop from my eyes. This really was Jesus. This really was our King. As the monstrance neared, I looked up at the Lord, and I prayed a simple prayer: "You are Christ, You are the King, I will do what You ask. I will go where You want." The young woman who prayed that prayer was nowhere near ready to enter a convent. I didn't even know how to find a convent! I just knew that if it was what God wanted — as in that Jesus who I had just seen move through that room and be adored and worshiped and heal people and change people (change me), then I would figure it out, even if that meant in baby steps. I had fallen in love. A seed had broken through the soil, and again, my feet had been washed.

Cardinal Ratzinger (later Pope Benedict XVI) wrote in his book *God Is Near Us*:

> This is the meaning of [Christ's] whole life and Passion:
> that he bends down to our dirty feet, to the dirt of humanity, and that in his greater love he washes us clean.
> The service of washing the feet was performed in order
> to prepare a person suitably for sitting at table, to make

him ready for company, so that all could sit down together for a meal. Jesus Christ prepares us, as it were, for God's presence and for each other's company, so that we can sit down together at table. We, who repeatedly find we cannot stand one another, who are quite unfit to be with God, are welcomed and accepted by him. He clothes himself, so to speak, in the garment of our poverty, and in being taken up by him, we are able to be with God, we have gained access to God. We are washed through our willingness to yield to his love.

"Our willingness to yield to his love." All those years before, when my friend knelt and washed my feet, I had yielded to love. The tears were a mixture of relief and grief. Grief as I let go of some of what Pope Benedict XVI describes in the same passage as the "pride of wanting to do it for myself," by which he is referring to manufacturing love on my own terms. That night, before the Blessed Sacrament, I yielded to love, and again, I felt relief and grief. Relief to accept Jesus as King, and grief surrendering my plans so that Christ's could reign.

I SEE MY RELATIONSHIP WITH JESUS IN THE EUCHARIST AS A LIFELONG YIELDING.

I see my relationship with Jesus in the Eucharist as a lifelong yielding. I think it is the lifelong part that is hard for each of us sometimes. We would like to skip ahead. We think, if this is really Jesus, if this is really God who has bowed down to wash me, cleanse me, heal me, and make me like himself in my reception of the Eucharist, why do I continue to make such a mess of it? I receive Jesus and then I continue to struggle with sin. I continue to be afraid. I continue to hesitate at times to move forward with the steps I have discerned that God is calling me to take and has also given me the graces to take. What is also true is that I continue to go to confession. I continue to go to Mass. I add some daily Masses. I keep trying. I keep growing. Bit by bit. Degree by degree. Fast is an illusion. Look at Scripture: Even when God healed, it wasn't a fairy tale happily ever after, the story is over now. The person was healed for mission and healed to be set on a journey. The healing was the beginning of an ongoing journey of healing and restoration. God didn't snap His fingers to free the Israelites from Egypt and voila, they are in the promised land. They walked! A lot! It was slow. That slow journey is the bulk of what we call Scripture, and it's lovely. The Eucharist is the ultimate slow game.

There have been many places in my life and in my heart that God has willed to heal slowly. I know that sometimes there can be immediate miraculous healings, and I do believe in those. I also believe that even those circumstances require slow work to adjust to the new reality. I have learned that my own disdain about the slowness of it all actually can at times diminish the beauty of the Lord abiding with me, and taking His time with me. There have been moments where I have found myself before the tabernacle asking the Lord, *Why so slow? Why so long? How are we still here?* And I have perceived the Lord in prayer offer me this response: *You underestimate the depth of your need for Me.*

One of the areas in my life that has helped me to enter into slow healing and let the Lord take His time is in my relationship with my birth mother. When I was seven years old, she had sent us to live with our father, who would in the next year take his own life. She was struggling with mental health issues, and after our father died, we did not return to her. Twenty-two years later, I would see her again. It was 2011, and I was preparing my application to enter with the sisters as a candidate. I was having monthly conversations over video conference with the vocations director as a part of my application and preparation, and one day during one of our monthly calls, she leaned a little closer to the screen and asked me if I was able to locate my mother. I knew I could. I knew she was still in Houston, but I was not open to the idea. The vocations director pressed further and inquired if I had thought of finding her to offer her forgiveness.

Two things came to my mind. One, I thought it was ridiculous to extend forgiveness to someone who had not asked for it. Two, as I told my therapist shortly after, I needed to take the vocations director off my trust list. I thought her recommendation was impossible and unnecessary. My therapist was a good one, and he helped me explore my feelings about the recommendation, and six weeks later, I called my birth mother and set up a time to meet. In the course of those six weeks, I had managed to puff myself up so much in my mind that the narrative I had about this upcoming meeting was that I was a minister going to help a broken woman. I was doing God's work. I even compiled an "I am gonna go minister to my mother" playlist for the drive into Houston. By the grace of God, as the day to meet my mother neared, God brought me low, but not in a bad way — in the best way. I decreased so that He might increase. Two days before our meeting, two of my family members apologized to me for mistakes they thought they made when I was a little girl. Their apologies brought me as a little girl to the forefront of my mind. The day before our meeting, I lost a necklace my best friend had entrusted to me to carry as I prepared to see my mother. The helplessness I felt as I looked for it reminded me of my vulnerability and lack of control. Finally, on the day of our meeting, as I prepared to leave the house, my uncle stopped me, and in the most loving and fatherly way asked if I was OK. I had not told him what I was going to do — he just knew something was going on with me. That was it. I yielded to his fatherly love and fell against his chest and sobbed, like a small girl.

By the time I sat down in front of my mother, I was right-sized. I was a daughter, a grieving daughter, a daughter seeking to forgive. Those of you who minister, I need you to hear me on this. Sometimes when we seek to minister, we get so in the way that Christ, who is the one we are *administering* to others, has no room to enter in. When I was right-sized before my mother, Christ was able to rule and reign in our encounter. It was beautiful. She was beautiful. She took notes! She said she likes to take notes during important conversations. At that table that day, I learned that it is never wasteful to extend forgiveness to someone who didn't ask for it. I got to hear my mother's story, and for the first time ever, I wanted to be like her. Before that moment, I had always been afraid when people told me that I was like her; it felt like a curse, like it meant her story would be my story. As she shared her story, all I heard was unshakable faith, this joy that had a lift and lightness to it, that was wise and firm and strong and enduring; and I let an unexpected prayer float through my mind: *God, I hope I inherit that from her.* She also, just months before I would enter religious life, confirmed my vocation. I told her about my plans to explore being a nun, and she looked dead on without a bit of surprise and said, "OK." I pointed out to her that she did not seem shocked, and she replied without a bit of hesitation that she always knew I had a different call from marriage, she just did not know what. She told me she would watch me play and interact with people and would say she did not know what it was, but that for this child, God had a different call.

My mother attended my first vows, where she told me she was so proud of me. Since then, we sometimes exchange calls, and we sometimes exchange letters, but we never really had that hallmark moment or a scene like the ones in the show *Full House*, where the music plays and all is perfect. In some ways, it is still awkward; there is a lot of brokenness there. Also, God is not done. The slow work of God is still in process. This does not undermine, diminish, or lessen what God has healed between my mother and me; nor does it detract from the beauty of what He has accomplished because there is still some ash mixed in with the beauty. In fact, it spurs on my hope for what one day might be, even if that one day is when the kingdom has fully come.

THE SLOW WORK OF GOD IS STILL IN PROCESS.

When I think about the first time I received the Eucharist at the Easter Vigil in 2005, and then all that has happened between that moment and my encounter with the Eucharist in 2009, and then from then until now, I can see it more clearly. All that scraping and crawling and walking and running forward, how God has slowly worked over time to transform me degree by degree into His likeness. And I am not claiming to be special; He is doing the same for my birth mother, for my family; He is doing the same for you. This is His promise to us in the Eucharist: to unite us to Him so closely that we become like Him. After all, as Saint Athanasius tells us, "He became man so that we might become God." This is our hope. Think about all that has occurred between the first time you received the Eucharist and today. List the ways you have grown in wisdom and stature and favor. List the ways you have been healed, even if there is still work to do in that area. Jesus is not slow with us because He needs to be slow. He is slow with us because *we* need this slowness. We need time to let it sink in, to take root, to get the hang of it.

This slowness is also a testament of God's love and desire for us. God isn't quickly done with us, stepping into our lives to heal us and then vanishing like a wizard. God is constant and enduring, and His slowness is a sign of how invested God is in His children and in the promise of His kingdom. For "we are God's children now; what we shall be has not yet been revealed. We do know that when it is revealed we shall be like him" (1 Jn

3:2), which takes time, and the slow work of God.

Sometimes, my frustration with the slowness of it all is connected to watching loved ones suffer and struggle, and longing for God to remove the suffering. I remember once I was struggling even more than was typical with this as I watched a relative I love very much relapse into his drug addiction. When I learned of the relapse, I stopped praying, and even when I did pray a little, I did not visit with God about my relative's relapse. I was angry. And then one night, I was back before a monstrance — just like that first night, now many years earlier. Jesus in the Blessed Sacrament was being worshiped and adored. It was clear that it was time to visit with Jesus about my relative, and my prayer that night was full of anger. I was very honest with Jesus in prayer. I told Him that I was afraid that my relative would die, alone and by overdose. I was afraid for the phone to ring and deliver that news. The fear left me feeling sick. And then I looked at Jesus in the Eucharist and asked in prayer: "There it is. There is everything I have not been saying. What could you possibly have to say that would be helpful? What?!" And then, I received the most unexpected perception in prayer. I perceived Jesus say, "I am sorry." And at that, I yielded, again, to love.

I went on in prayer to come to understand that my relationship with Jesus is not about Jesus fixing things for me; that was never the promise. The promise was presence, Emmanuel. God says to us that He will be with us. This presence is so profound and transforming that the true healing isn't about fixing the sufferings and painful circumstances in our lives. Do not get me wrong, in the end He will wipe away every tear from our eyes. But the true healing is that we are being made to be like Him. He is so close, so near, so intimate, that we will become Him: a marriage, one flesh. This is our only sure hope. Jesus. Everything else will fade. Even hope itself will fade, and only He will remain. Somehow, then, this slow work becomes the greatest romance there ever was, the greatest adventure there ever was. The slowness is not a threat to the promise, but instead a reason to delight that the promise stands even when life is slow and ordinary and difficult and awkward. Constantly, God is reaching down and washing our feet, inviting us time and time again to yield to this love until we have yielded so much that we are transformed into this Love. With every reception of the Eucharist, we yield to this Love.

Sometimes, it is hard to know what being transformed by and into this Love looks like in real life. We can always refer to the lives of the saints for that. When we forgive; when we sacrifice; when we go back and try again in relationships where it is healthy to keep trying; when we apologize: All of these experiences are the fruit of the presence and effect of the Eucharist in our lives. There is a poem I love about my martyred Sisters of Nowogrodek, Sr. Mary Stella and her Ten Companions, Sisters of the Holy Family of Nazareth, that I have always felt explained this perfectly, this transformation. They were martyred during World War II in modern-day Belarus. They were taken prisoner by Nazi soldiers and detained for one night, most likely undergoing questioning regarding the location of the town priest, and then in the early morning they were led into the woods, shot one by one, and buried in a common grave. They sacrificed their lives for the men in the village, whom the Nazi soldiers had also taken prisoner, and for the priest of the village. The author of this poem is one of our sisters, anonymous, and I believe if at this point you are not quite sure what the slow work

MY RELATIONSHIP WITH JESUS IS NOT ABOUT JESUS FIXING THINGS FOR ME; THAT WAS NEVER THE PROMISE. THE PROMISE WAS PRESENCE, EMMANUEL.

of God is in each of us in the Eucharist, what we really long,
yearn, and hope for, then perhaps this poem will help:

> A holy silence continued in the forest
> as though in a chapel,
> beneath the shade of pine-stained glass,
> before the altar of love
> eleven white Hosts:
> eleven recollected faces …
> Trees over them engrossed in prayer
> are singing the antiphon
> for the entrance …
>
> The Holy Sacrifice has begun …
> In a little while
> the call of the silver bell
> will ring out the quiet moment
> for the offering.
> No … this is not a bell:
> the silence was broken sadly
> by shots …
> signs of steel
> scattered the silence of dawn:
>
> the sign of offering.
> O blessed death
> you receive the sacrificial gift
> in your cold earthen arms
> and give them back to the Lord —
> Paten of bloody sacrifice.
>
> O earth soaked with purple blood,
> earth silent and quiet,

this blood is to flow with Christ's
into a shared chalice.
Ite missa est …
My dear Sisters,
your sacrifice is ended,
already your love
stretched on the Cross
on the shared Cross
of eleven arms.
Go,
your sacrifice was accepted.

I would add only one thing. The sacrifice *is* accepted, the sacrifices that come with each and every yielding. They establish the reign of God in the world as King, and they serve to usher in the Resurrection.

8

OUR RESURRECTION: WE WILL BE LIKE HIM

When the faithful receive the Body of the Son, they proclaim to one another the Good News that the first fruits of life have been given, as when the angel said to Mary Magdalene, "Christ is risen!" Now too are life and resurrection conferred on whoever receives Christ.

— *CCC 1391*

The Resurrection is at work in each one of us, and in the world, bringing about a likeness to Christ so that in the end, the sign of His reign will be that all things are like Him. I did not fully grasp the primacy of this teaching until I had what would be the second most meaningful confession of my life thus far.

I was now a religious sister, studying to be a counselor and attending my first conference for Catholic counselors. I had been hesitant to attend because I had stereotyped counselors who practice from a faith perspective as having a tendency to use faith as an excuse for clinical laziness. I was wrong. The conference was exceptional and full of people living the "both/and" beautifully, practicing from a perspective steeped in faith and also clinically disciplined. The conference offered a day of retreat in the beginning, and I participated, wanting to take it all in. It was led by a priest who served in the ministry of exorcism, and as I listened to him, I believed that this man would one day be a saint. He was older (in his early nineties), and for a time in his life had had Padre Pio as a confessor. He had also served Mother Teresa as a retreat director and spiritual guide. I loved the way he spoke about the hearts of Jesus and Mary, about the reign of those hearts in the world, and because he had so much Catholic street cred, I was hoping to make my confession with him. I eventually got the opportunity. We sat down (he was reluctant, because I caught him at a time when he had not planned to hear confessions, but he relented in the face of my pushiness), and I made my confession. He looked at me when I finished and told me that I had one sin, and then he paused for a long, dramatic moment. *What?!* I thought. Finally, he told me my one struggle was a lack of trust in God's providence. I had to agree with that as a primary struggle at the root of most of my sin. He went on to ask me an important question: "Do you believe that when the Father looks at you, He sees Jesus?" I now took my own long pause, and then I responded as honestly as possible: "I think that is something I would like to believe."

WHEN THE FATHER LOOKS AT ME, HE SEES JESUS.

I left that confession and pondered this truth for weeks:

When the Father looks at me, He sees Jesus. At first, it honestly sounded like heresy. But then, by chance, I picked up *Ecclesia de Eucharistia* by Pope St. John Paul II and read this:

> Even when it is celebrated on the humble altar of a country church, the Eucharist is always in some way celebrated *on the altar of the world.* It unites heaven and earth. It embraces and permeates all creation. The Son of God became man in order to restore all creation, in one supreme act of praise, to the One who made it from nothing. He, the Eternal High Priest who by the blood of his Cross entered the eternal sanctuary, thus gives back to the Creator and Father all creation redeemed. He does so through the priestly ministry of the Church, to the glory of the Most Holy Trinity. Truly this is the *mysterium fidei* which is accomplished in the Eucharist: the world which came forth from the hands of God the Creator now returns to him redeemed by Christ. (8)

In that passage, I saw the explanation for this truth, that when the Father looks at each of us, He sees Jesus. How could He not? The Body, Blood, Soul, and Divinity of Jesus permeates all of creation as a result of the Blood of the cross of Jesus Christ. All has been covered in His Blood and handed back to the Father, able to be reconciled in the one who has covered us in himself. By the Blood of the cross (that covers each one of us), how could the Father not look at us and see Jesus, who has conferred the Resurrection on each one of us? I was thrilled to be able to embrace this truth. The Resurrection is at work in me, and because of the life, death, Resurrection, and ascension of Jesus, when the Father looks at me, he sees Jesus.

In the later years of my formation as a religious sister, as I prepared for final vows, being a woman of hope slowly transformed into embracing a spirituality of the Resurrection. I can look now and see that this spiritual focus was coming all along. When I submitted my application to be an affiliate with the sisters, the first stage of formation, the Scripture passage that my letter of request focused on was Isaiah 55:10–11:

> Yet just as from the heavens
> > the rain and snow come down
> And do not return there
> > till they have watered the earth,
> > making it fertile and fruitful,
> Giving seed to the one who sows
> > and bread to the one who eats,
> So shall my word be
> > that goes forth from my mouth;
> It shall not return to me empty,
> > but shall do what pleases me,
> > achieving the end for which I sent it.

In prayer, I now see this Scripture as a look to the Resurrection, and it is Jesus who now has watered the earth, making it fertile and fruitful and returning it full and pleasing to the Father. Jesus' very flesh is the bread that has come down from heaven.

Later in the novitiate, one day in prayer during Holy Week, my imagination was flooded with an image that has never left me and which also alluded to this spirituality of the Resurrection taking shape in me. It was a Good Friday image, colorless in my imagination. The sky was dark gray, the light so dim that the crosses on which Jesus and the two criminals crucified with Him hung appeared black. In the image rain was falling from the sky, drenching the earth. Yet beneath the soil — far beneath the soil — in prayer I saw a garden filled with sunlight and blooming flowers. Right there, beneath the storm of Calvary, were its fruits, the cross making the world fertile and fruitful. This garden grew toward bursting through the surface. Later, after first vows, this idea continued to take shape.

I had another experience in prayer, one that it would take years for God to unfold and for me to see its connection to this spirituality of the Resurrection forming in me. I was on my annual retreat about two years after first vows, and I was handed a meditation to use in prayer that day from the Ignatian tradition. The best way to share it with you is to invite you to do it. You might set aside about twenty minutes for this meditation.

It is important in this reflection that you do not read ahead. At one point you will be asked to stop reading and sit in prayer with the instructions you have received so far and not read ahead. Imagine you are in an empty room, a place where you are going to make a statue or a sculpture. Imagine that you are gathering up supplies to make a sculpture and begin creating a sculpture of yourself. In your imagination, in prayer, create a sculpture that represents the way you think God sees you. Now pause and spend some time praying with what you have created. Do not read ahead until you feel as though you are ready to move ahead in prayer.

Now, imagine that Jesus walks into the room, and you watch as He begins to make a second sculpture next to the one you made. Imagine Jesus is making a sculpture next to your sculpture of how He sees you. How are the two sculptures the same? How are they each different? Reflect on the similarities and the differences and your thoughts and feelings about them.

When I did this reflection on annual retreat, the first statue — the one I made — was of an adult woman, who appeared lovely and regal (of course). She was made of colorless white clay, and she appeared tall and serious. (Mind you, I am neither!) When Jesus entered the room in my prayer, He made an entirely different statue. He made a statue of a little girl, whose hair was in ponytails with barrettes on them. She had a huge smile on her. The statue was full of color, and she appeared to be running. The differences broke my heart. That's all I knew at that time, was that the differences broke my heart. It would be a few years before I learned the relationship between this time in prayer and the spirituality of the Resurrection taking shape in me.

Years later, I was on a thirty-day retreat, which was a part of my preparation for final vows. It was during the pandemic, not long after George Floyd's murder and the righteous anger that erupted in our country afterward. Thirty days of silence including four hours of daily prayer couldn't come too soon. During those days, I prayed through the full spiritual exercises of Saint Ignatius, which is prayer steeped in Scripture. I was able to reflect on the corporate nature of sin by reading the newspaper during the portions of the exercises devoted to prayer about personal and corporate sin. I walked, in prayer, with the Holy Family through the early years of Jesus' life. I prayed through the Scriptures that gave the accounts of Jesus' public ministry. I journeyed through the passion with the Blessed Virgin as my guide, and this is where I believe a Resurrection spirituality broke forth above the soil in me. As I shared before, now having a loving relationship with the Blessed Virgin, I was with Mary at the foot of the cross in an extended time of prayer, returning to the cross for each prayer period over the course of two days. In prayer, we laid Jesus in the tomb, and the stone was placed to close the tomb. In prayer, I imagined Mary walking around in the garden where the tomb had been hewn. As I prayed, it seemed to me that Mary was tending the garden around the tomb and waiting as she tended.

The last reflection in the spiritual exercises comes pretty quickly after praying with the Resurrection, and as I shared previously, it is titled "Contemplation to Attain the Love of God." It is a prayer reflection not on obtaining God's love, because that is not something we achieve, but rather on learning to love like God with a response of love to the love we have received. The retreatant is invited to pray about four key points: one, that I am created out of love by God; two, that I have been given many natural and supernatural gifts out of this love, including the sacraments of the Church, which are a sign of God's desire to dwell in me; three, that God works tirelessly for me, and in me, as a gardener works in his garden; and lastly, that all, everything, is a gift. Throughout the meditation, the retreatant is invited to pray for the graces to respond to this love with love, and to serve the mission of Jesus Christ. The retreatant asks for the grace to have an intimate knowledge of the many blessings that have been received throughout the retreat, in order to be filled with gratitude and have the courage to love and serve God joyfully.

> *JESUS WANTS TO RAISE EVERYTHING TO LIFE, IN HIM. US, THIS WORLD, OUR LOVED ONES, OUR ENEMIES, OUR STRUGGLES, OUR SUFFERINGS, OUR LOSSES, OUR WOUNDS.*

I had prayed with the resurrected Lord and was now ready to pray the "Contemplation to Attain the Love of God." I sat down and oriented myself to prayer, asking the Holy Spirit to help me to pray, calling on the saints for their intercession (as we never pray alone), and settling into the meditation by reading the reflection that had been given to me. I closed my eyes. I shared with you before that when I met Jesus in that meditation, I was a little girl, but here is how we arrived there. The first thing

I imagined in the prayer was being back in the room from my prayer years earlier, with my statue and the statue Jesus made. I was shocked by this, but I remained in prayer, continuing to call on the Holy Spirit for help. In prayer, I perceived Jesus destroying the statue I had made. It shattered. Then I imagined the little girl statue he had made in prayer all those years before coming to life. In my contemplation to attain the love of God, the key image was this little girl version of myself, alive through, with, and in the resurrected Jesus, running ahead in the world, alongside Jesus, sowing seeds of the Resurrection with each step. Full of joy with each step. Full of confidence with each step. Hers was a confidence not rooted in circumstances or dependent upon happiness, but upon the utterly un-circumstantial Jesus. Jesus wants to raise everything to life, in Him. Us, this world, our loved ones, our enemies, our struggles, our sufferings, our losses, our wounds. And once we are raised to life, He wants us to press inward, onward, and upward on His behalf, spreading His kingdom, spreading the love that abides between the Father and himself in the Trinity with the Spirit, in the ordinary circumstances of our lives.

When I was becoming a counselor, I chose to specialize in trauma. I was attracted to healing trauma within a couple of weeks of my first course on the topic. But I was confused about why. Why would I choose a specialty riddled with darkness? I am not the martyr type! Over time I learned that healing trauma gave me a front-row seat to some of the most beautiful work that the resurrected Jesus is doing in this world through His Spirit. So often, trauma includes a person having experiences that are utterly contrary to the dignity of a human person and what the human person was created for. This is due to sin and brokenness in the world. This is precisely what Jesus rose to restore. As a counselor helping people heal from trauma, I get to witness the empty tomb on a regular basis.

My most recent progression in growing in a spirituality of the Resurrection has been in my reflections on Mary Magdalene and on six key words about her written in Scripture: "She bent over into the tomb" (Jn 20:11). She intentionally entered the tomb. She went looking about in a place of death, where she should have found stench and sorrow, and instead she discovered eternal life. In this she became an usher of the Resurrection, the Apostle to the Apostles. An image of her that I purchased from the Museum of the Bible, which depicts the empty tomb full of light at her heart, hangs in my counseling office. As a counselor, I have been able to hone this spirituality of the Resurrection that was born in becoming a woman of hope. We are ushers of the Resurrection that has been conferred upon us. As ushers of the Resurrection, running ahead alongside Jesus, sowing seeds of the Resurrection, we are not preoccupied with seemingly lovely places. No, we stoop down into tombs, because we know that in hope they can be made places of life. We can sit silently with someone who grieves, not paralyzed with the worry of searching for the perfect words. We can personally engage a person who is dealing with poverty without fear that we will not be enough, will not have enough, or will be asked for what feels like too much. We can go back into relationships where it is safe and healthy to do so and apologize, forgive, and seek reconciliation. Hope can feel like a problem precisely because it needs a tomb to be what it is and do what it will do. But in Jesus, the problem is solved. Death is conquered, and life is eternal. Light casts out darkness, and suffering gains meaning and value. In this rests our hope. In *Evangelii Gaudium*, Pope Francis encourages us

> *HOPE CAN FEEL LIKE A PROBLEM PRECISELY BECAUSE IT NEEDS A TOMB TO BE WHAT IT IS AND DO WHAT IT WILL DO.*

to recall that we should not wait until we feel we have it all together to go forth and evangelize. He notes that we are evangelized as we evangelize. So it is with being an usher of the Resurrection. As we help invite others into the light of the Resurrection, so we also stoop down into the tombs in our own lives seeking signs of the Resurrection.

I remember being in the throes of work with my first therapist. I was still working in banking and discerning religious life. One of the things I struggled with at that time was not accepting the scathing nature of the wound of abandonment that I had experienced — especially abandonment that included my father's suicide. I found myself doing that thing we can sometimes do in therapy where we are digging around for repressed memories, more wounds, or some other unknown, abstract pain. Surely there has to be something even more painful to explain why I am in so much emotional pain. I believe this is actually well-laid resistance to facing the obvious and concrete pain right before us. It was so hard for me to show myself compassion and accept that abandonment is in fact scathingly painful. There didn't have to be more to explain how much pain I was in. It was also hard for me to show myself compassion and accept that abandonment wasn't the whole reason I was dealing with emotional pain; there was some of it that I had caused myself, through my own poor adult choices. Part of my work with my therapist at that time included looking earnestly not only at my past, but also at my family's past. I came to better understand my brothers' perspectives and the perspectives of my mom and dad, of my aunt and uncle, and also of that eight-year-old little girl who looked up one night and did not have parents. Somewhere in there, I also came to better understand the perspective of myself in the present, a young woman at that time in her late twenties. One night, I decided to call my oldest brother and ask him if there was anything I didn't know — more that had happened to us that I did not remember. I stooped down further into the tomb. I will never forget that conversation and what I found there when I stooped down and went in, and looked closer. It was like a litany of love. He simply said, "Toni, what I remember and what I want you to remember is that you were and have always been so loved." He went on to give testimony to all the little and ordinary ways my father had loved me, that my mother had loved me, that my middle brother had loved me, and how he himself had loved me. As he spoke, my senses were filled with these memories of love. And I yielded to it. And I let that tomb fill with light. And I let another part of myself be transformed into the likeness of Christ through Resurrection hope.

I want to say the same to you now. I do not know your story. I do not know whose hands this book will land in. But I can say with great assurance that you too are and have always been so loved; and I have the great privilege of being an usher of this love, to encourage you to remember it, to hold onto it as readily as we tend to hold on to wounds — if not more readily. It can be hard to believe, especially if you have suffered or are suffering. But as sure as the breath that just filled your lungs, so sure is this love. And because of the life, death, and Resurrection of Jesus, in the end, we will be like Him, and His love will reign in the world. Until then, let us place our hope in Him (see Ps 33:22). Now, I will leave you with one of the most important questions I have ever been asked: What is your greatest hope?

ACT OF HOPE

Hope is one the three theological virtues: faith, hope, and love. The difference between these virtues and all the other virtues is that we do not work to achieve them; they are instead infused into our souls at baptism by God to help us live as His children. The *Catechism of the Catholic Church* reads, "They are the pledge of the presence and action of the Holy Spirit in the faculties of the human being" (1813). As a theological virtue, hope has been given to us by God, and it is a sign that God lives in us and acts in us, and has not abandoned us.

If you are needing to be strengthened in hope, in this pledge that God has not left us orphans, you can pray an Act of Hope:

O Lord God,
I hope by your grace for the pardon
of all my sins
and after life here to gain eternal happiness
because You have promised it
who are infinitely powerful, faithful, kind,
and merciful.

In this hope I intend to live and die.
Amen.

BIBLIOGRAPHY

Barron, Robert. *Catholicism: A Journey to the Heart of the Faith.* New York: Image Books, 2011.

Francis. *Evangelii Gaudium.* November 24, 2013. Vatican.va.

———. Angelus. November 1, 2017. Vatican.va.

John Paul II. *Ecclesia de Eucharistia.* April 17, 2003. Vatican.va.

———. General Audience. November 11, 1998. Vatican.va.

Paul VI. *Gaudium et Spes.* December 7, 1965. Vatican.va.

Ratzinger, Joseph. *God Is Near Us: The Eucharist, the Heart of Life.* Edited by Stephan Otto Horn and Vinzenz Pfnür. Translated by Henry Taylor. San Francisco: Ignatius Press, 2003.

Sarah, Robert. "Herald Top 10: Cardinal Sarah: 'As a Bishop, It Is My Duty to Warn the West.'" *Catholic Herald.* December 31, 2019.

https://catholicherald.co.uk/herald-top-10-cardinal-sarah-as-a-bishop-it-is-my-duty-to-warn-the-west/.

ABOUT THE AUTHOR

Sr. Josephine Garrett, CSFN, is a native Texan, born and raised in Houston. She earned a BA in politics with a business concentration from the University of Dallas and then worked for ten years in the banking industry. She entered the Catholic Church in 2005, and in November 2011, began her formation to be a religious sister with the Sisters of the Holy Family of Nazareth. She professed first vows in October 2015, and subsequently served in marketing for her religious community's retreat center and vocations ministry while earning a master's degree in clinical mental health counseling. She professed her final vows in November 2020. Sister now serves as a licensed mental health counselor, a nationally certified counselor, specializing in trauma and child and adolescent counseling. She is a national speaker.